The Devil

DISGUISED AS A

Jesus-Loving Lesbian

AGATHA SLOANE

WESTBOW
PRESS®
A DIVISION OF THOMAS NELSON
& ZONDERVAN

WestBow Press books may be ordered through booksellers or by contacting:

WestBow Press
A Division of Thomas Nelson & Zondervan
1663 Liberty Drive
Bloomington, IN 47403
www.westbowpress.com
844-714-3454

ISBN: 978-1-6642-6916-3 (sc)
ISBN: 978-1-6642-6915-6 (hc)
ISBN: 978-1-6642-6917-0 (e)

Library of Congress Control Number: 2022911169

Print information available on the last page.

WestBow Press rev. date: 7/13/2022

Contents

Acknowledgments

Mom, thank you for being a living example of God's meekness, long-suffering, and disproportionate patience.

Dad, thank you for being ever willing and for faithfully enduring pain, continuously convicting me of the gravity in remaining receptive to discipline.

My siblings, thank you for refusing to accept a fraudulent version of me and for being a source of consistency and light along my way.

Mom-mom, thank you for standing in kind and patient resistance to my detestable behavior.

Grandmom, thank you for helping me realize that admitting I was wrong was the strongest act I could ever achieve.

Mary, thank you for welcoming me in when nobody else would, for feeding me when I was hungry and nurturing me when I was sick.

Thank you, Wonderful Counselor, Prince of Peace, for loving me first. Thank you for the ears to hear your voice, for the eyes to the see the worthiness of your Spirit's wisdom. Bless your name, for you gave me more than what I was searching for; you gave me an unshakeable love and reverence for you, which in turn has generated a natural love and adoration for humanity, whom you created in your sovereign image. Thank you for all of the faith-filled people you've placed along my path. Thank you for dying the brutal and agonizing death I deserved for my hard heart posture and patiently guiding me back to your loving arms. Your benevolent discipline delights me.

Who the Son sets free is free indeed.

Introduction

Lies. We all tell them or participate in them at one point or another. Not only do we place our trust in their promise to make difficult situations easier, we also place our hope in their pledge to hide the truth we would prefer to go unexposed. We take dependable liberty with these lies because we deem ourselves their creator, determining which lies are harmless and which are justifiably necessary. And when our artistic distortion of truth fails to procure the results we desire, we thoughtfully propagate blame as a secondary shield from what we cannot bare to be revealed. Lies provide the soil where images and false realities are planted, watered, and humanly modified.

The brands we become determine who we are and what we want to be known as. Much like commodity consumer products, we are virtually the same, with a few unique features that distinguish us from one another. We give birth to identity when we begin to claim those features as our own, as if we ourselves created ourselves. Whether it be our gender, our body type, our nation of origin, or the pigment of our largest organ, we claim what we have not made and worship self-refined images of who we think we would rather be. We glorify rebellion and vilify reverence. We set the standards for right and wrong. We deem the measures for justice and vengeance. We judge civilization and proclaim what is best for coexistence. We define love and portray the Creator in our image. We crave control and then criticize God when things don't go our way. Our behavior toward one another and the state of this world demonstrates that we simply cannot stand the thought of surrendering our own ideals for the fear of our Lord.

Lies. That's where all of this started. Like the original humans created in the garden, I heard a whisper that caused me to doubt God. As life continued on, with heartbroken cries unanswered, I made a choice to heed a voice that spoke directly to my needs and wants. I didn't know the questions to be deceitful at the time; they were far too practical and applicable to seem dangerous. I also did not know the state of my heart condition, assuming emotions were the light posts to my life, all of which made faith seem more like a privilege for those with fewer problems. I couldn't afford to not see the full staircase, so I developed a brand of my own and set off to build each step—without God.

Albeit a true story, it is not for the faint of heart. I am writing from a unique perspective as a follower of Christ in the freest country in the world. I am not a theological scholar, rather a seminary dropout. I grew up in the institutional church community, never obtaining my longing for a sense of belonging. I recognize that in many other places I could be imprisoned for some of the things I confess here, furthermore killed for acknowledging Jesus as my Savior and King. Before meeting Jesus, there was not one commandment that I did not disobey. Even murder, while not committed physically, was an equally rotten seed of anger in my heart. My experience with love felt far from God's portrayal in 1 Corinthians 13. Love was tumultu-ous, initiated by pas-sion and fueled by jealousy and envy. Love was unrepentant and expectant of infinite forgiveness. Love demanded reparation, fighting valiantly for it. There was no place for humility and selflessness in love; those positions were too weak and vulnerable. Love thrived on dramatic, relational vandalism that thwarted separation then sought half-hearted apologies in an effort to consume it again. Love naturally accompanied hate as a love within a love for the adrenaline rush of winning, of proving the distorted reality of love we chose was the true one. Love is what happens to us, what makes us think and act irrationally. Love didn't have the power to change, let alone transform. It was too fleeting of an emotion to even last that long.

And yet love is what we all chase after. We all want to be loved for the worst, most shame-filled parts of ourselves. We all want someone who will adore our good qualities and tolerate our dark ones. We don't think there is a need to change when it comes to love; if someone truly loves us unconditionally, they will take us just as we are. We want true love yet choose a debauched, volatile version of it instead. Despite our choice, we blame government and other powers for the love we have declared, deflecting accountability for our current state of divide and hate. Love is blind and crazy. Tornadoes of dissolution and displacement should be expected. How easy it is to remain unrepentant when love is so fluid, when we set the barometer for right and wrong.

I used my gifts and talents as a means to my own ends and still expected love as result. I've heard that's the definition of insanity, doing the same thing over and over, expecting a different result. To wake up and realize that what you've become best at is utterly corrupt is nothing short of devastating. I cannot speak about the topics of sin or repentance without acknowledging that or without identifying myself as the greatest sinner and most civilized monster around. I lived most of my life claiming to know God without ever reading a page of scripture. Safe to say, I was also the biggest hypocrite. Attending a building called church was one of the masks I wore to appear good. The messages were often inspiring; however, I was never moved to change. I met God through Jesus, who first met me in the dark alleys, where the betrayal of those lies left me. He didn't condemn my complicit allegiance to deceit, nor did he shame me for forfeiting the Good News for money and promiscuous power. He convicted my heart with a hunger for true love, for a determination to know the truth about God. That search started with a friend, who I desired to love in the purest and cleanest of ways. It was becoming evident that my ways of love were poisonous, which made every attempt at demonstrating love confusing. So I set off on a mission to meet the author of love, because I needed to know the truth directly from the one who defined it. I needed to know who I was directly from the one who created me. I needed to know that there was a purpose for humanity, directly from the one who designed it. I needed to know that there was more to it all, that life was not just about surviving for a short while and then dying. I knocked, and the door was opened to me.

I wrote these letters when I decided that I didn't want to lie anymore, when I decided that I didn't want to waste one more minute living out death's mission. I was praying fervently, in constant conversation with God. I had discerned that seminary was not the right place for me and that I was being called to be a disciple in the world. The desire to be a servant for Christ was all I wanted, to glorify him for his good and faithful ways. While that prompting brought great peace to my heart, it also delivered deep conviction. Everyone I knew in my old life had abandoned me when I started making different life choices. When I chose the gym over the bar, I lost all of my so-called bar friends. When I chose studying my Bible at night and a healthier sleep routine over late nights out in the city, I lost all of my city acquaintances. I couldn't find a single soul to relate to what I was going through. Addie was the only one who tried to understand. Despite the fact that we couldn't seem to make a real, authentic connection for the entirety of our relationship, neither of us stopped trying. As the Word would teach me, that is a sign of true love. It never gives up.

I was willing to do whatever it took to love her purely, even if I died trying to figure out what that meant. I wrote these letters in an effort to expose the lies, the masks I wore to uphold the lies, and the deceitful images I portrayed into the world in the name of love. I wrote them as a testimony to the untrustworthy disposition our hearts are born with and as a testimony to the need for a new heart only Jesus can provide. I lied to Addie about everything. I hurt everyone I loved, and more. I believed the lies that told me the vigorous chains around my heart were protecting me, shielding my vulnerable fears and shame. All they did was keep people out and keep God at a distance. I never got the chance to explain, to repent, or to ask for her forgiveness. These are the everyday sins that keep us apart—and the inconceivable love freely available should we truly decide to unite.

Resuscitate

Dear Addie, may this note find you well.

I'm sure I am the last person you'd like to be receiving a letter from. I wouldn't go as far as to say that things were left undone, as it was pretty clear where each of us stood. The thing is that I was not completely honest in my stance. And not a day has gone by since that I don't regret not having spoken the truth to you. Lying to anyone about who you are is probably the most destructive act one can commit in a relationship. Lying to someone you love is worse, I think, and should be classified as a heinous act, as it carries the same power to assassinate as any physical means. Six years of an on-and-off-again relationship followed by four years of silence leads me to believe you have no appetite for an explanation. I have one for you, though, because there were too many things I left unsaid, too many questions I left unanswered. Regardless of time or how we left things when we did, I will never stop loving you. And if I've learned anything from all of this, it is that love never gives up.

That was probably the most confusing part of it all—how two people can say they love each other yet behave as if they exist in a universe outside of the definition. It makes sense to me now that your final words to me were "Stop being so angry." I can assume a thousand reasons why you thought I was angry, assuredly none as burdensome as the real one. Perhaps this is why choosing to tell the truth can be so liberating. It's a perilous battle to take a stand against every person, persuasion, and promise that has ever threatened to suppress who you really are and what you really love. It demands ruthless courage to speak the words that once spoken cannot ever be unheard. Surviving the anticipation that causes your heart to pound out of your chest, your lungs to restrict air, and your mind to devastatingly doubt, you're pulled toward the one moment for which you've been subconsciously desperate to arrive. The most distinctive and undeniably mandatory choice: life or death. That was where I was when we left it.

Maybe if I had continued the lie, we would still be some sort of friends. I wholeheartedly considered that against carrying on the predictability of deception, being accepted for everything I wasn't while simultaneously bearing the weight of never being known or loved for who I truly am. I was facing the greatest decision I never knew I had to make: to disown everything I thought I knew without knowing who or what I was going to lose. Tell me the truth—when you looked me in the eyes, did you not see a life tearing at the seams? Because I literally could not bear to live anymore. I was angry with the choices I had made. I was furious with the utter emptiness of false promises. And I deeply despised your loose use of the word *love* when you were nowhere to be found whenever I actually needed you. It's easy to mouth the words "I love you" and "I will always be there for you," until it requires something valuable from you, something sacrificial, to live it out. My foundation was crumbling, and this convenient, consumptive version of love was proving to be the source of the quake. I was suffocating and slipping, slowly coming to the realization that love was both the murderer and savior.

Lacking the emotional capacity to explain, I said goodbye in a text message. When a cold and distant communication didn't faze you after all we had been through together, my anger turned to sheer sadness. I withheld the truth all these years because I knew it would have meant losing you from the start. It happened anyway, just like everything else I had compromised myself for. We were always worlds apart, orbiting around the same curiosity: why I loved you in an infinitely indescribable way. I conceded with the realization that the root of the love I wanted to give was not the love you were looking to receive. I don't blame you, if that's what you're thinking. I am writing to you because I take full responsibility for my part. You had your secrecies, yet you were nothing if not consistently firm and transparent in your stance. The fact that I silently disagreed with everything you said and did while cowering as the victim and drowning in my own pile of brokenness was the furthest character from undying devotion. My love was clearly not pure; in fact, there was something wrong with it, like a disease that mortally wounded the hearts of everyone who came in contact with it.

"I am sorry" does not offer justice to years of that kind of blatant disrespect to love, which brings me to the very purpose of these letters. I will be writing to you with the truth of it all. I am by no means a writer or claim to have any special way with words. I simply promise to do my best to communicate what I could not before, hoping you have room in your heart to receive what I never got to say.

With peace and gratitude,
Chole

Whisper of Doubt

Dear Addie, may this note find you well.

There was a lot we never talked about. It seemed like the only subjects that weren't off-limits were food, music, and work. Maybe because they were predictably agreeable topics that did not threaten to penetrate the surface of our fragile spirits, unlike family and religion—we both had walls higher than one could climb in those areas. I cannot say for certain what foundation you built your heart on; I just knew I constructed mine with a sturdy lack of trust. Growing up, I didn't have a protected space to let my guard down or a single soul I felt safe sharing my stories with. I saw the world through a cruel lens, one that was superficial, belligerent, and unforgiving. Maybe that's why I didn't give much thought to what I wanted to do when I grew up; I was too preoccupied with who I wanted to be. I had an idea, and it came from a tiny one-by-two note I had tacked to a corkboard in my bedroom. The note read: "The fruit of the Spirit is love, joy, peace, forbearance, kindness, goodness, faithfulness, gentleness and self-control" (Galatians 5:22–23). The thought of living like that and embodying those characteristics captivated me. However, the reality of it, albeit vivid, existed only in my dreams.

For years, I watched arguments dictate much of the communication between the people in love in my life. On any given night throughout my adolescence, you could almost guarantee the sound of struggle echoing outside of our windows. Of many unforgettable altercations, there was one that stood out among the rest. I was about eight years old, hiding in my bedroom with the door slightly cracked open, eavesdropping on a dreadful exchange between my parents. The topics of these arguments were never well defined, yet what was always clear was the play on derogatory descriptors that aimed to destroy the other's sense of identity and self-worth. Accompanying the heartfelt insults were sounds of terrified tears and tormenting intimidation. A psychological opinion would verify that this type of warfare lends itself to conclude in pattern: threats of abandonment followed by physical destruction, which, in our house, manifested in normalized threats of divorce just prior to abstract assaults on household goods. The trouble with psychological opinion is that it focuses on an understanding of the actions derived from thoughts and emotions and utterly fails to acknowledge the roots in the heart that cause such relational vandalism.

Pondering matters of the heart was not something I found other third graders talking about, but I just knew without a shadow of a doubt that these battles were spiritual. Since saying that out loud felt like the fastest way to get made fun of or beat up, I kept quiet. I was captivated by a vision that displayed people apart from their behavior. Merely knowing there was an invisible divide didn't alleviate the deeply disturbing feeling about the choice to engage in it. Something was lurking around, inconspicuous to the eye yet fully exposed, with one clear intent: to kill love. That was as much as I could gather at the time, that love had an opposition. I couldn't stand the thought, especially after seeing how whatever it was had such power to slither in and turn even a simple conversation from civil to spiteful. I wanted to fight it, to expose its ugliness and lies. So much so that I started to find myself running toward conflict. I jumped into the middle of fights at school, fights about race and social status, fights between bullies and victims twice my size, some even with weapons. The passion I had at home was different though; I had a sense of vigorous urgency to act. I had this undeniable love for all people, which seemed to naturally be accompanied by pain from division and violence. Despite my family's flaws, there was a root of love that was unbreakable. The potential for it to be great was there; however, it could not seem to break from the plague of an entanglement with a diseased vine. It's maddening for me to see people hurting and do nothing about it—as if I could unsee it.

Anger in my household left a blast radius of tears and fears with each emotional explosion. I attacked back with what I had because I didn't have any other kind of weaponry at my disposal. I thought the presence of my youthful innocence between the firefight of word bullets would cause someone to stop and realize what they were doing. I thought it would open their eyes to the love they were so carelessly crushing. Except, each time I intervened, my plan resulted in the exact opposite of my intent. I met mockery, not peace. I was seen as the antagonist, targeted as the regime of resistance that required immediate eradication. I was a little girl who knew nothing about anything. Furthermore, as I was told, I knew nothing about God, whose name I leveraged in numerous failed attempts to muscle my message on love. I just couldn't bear to sit by and do nothing. I was on a mission to make them see that there was a better way to live. Such epiphany obviously did not happen in that moment; that night ended rather bitterly. My father threw me against the wall, like I was a crumpled up paper ball. My back hit the corner of the windowsill, and I slunk to the floor, where my mother was mopping up the debris and reminding me through her weakened voice with tear-filled face of my unwelcome engagement.

Feeling absolutely helpless, I ran back up the stairs, bruised and defeated. As I stood in the doorway, recalling the countless nights before this one and the innumerable nights to follow, I wrestled with one thought: *God can change this.* I gently closed my door and shut off the lights, sobbing and praying, praying and pleading. I knew in my heart that Jesus's love was immeasurably greater than the reckless display of love otherwise all around me. I didn't have much basis for that truth other than its undeniable residence in my heart. I knelt at my bedside with a tear-soaked face, sweating in prayerful solicitation while the halls echoed endlessly with profanity. As the early-morning hours approached with no peace in sight, I grew impatient and infuriated. I remember thinking, *Where is God? Why is there no change in my circumstances? Is he even listening?* And that's when I heard it. A voice so faint, like a thought far back in the mind. A soft whisper of a question perfectly aligned with the agony in my heart: *does God really care about you?*

I was kneeling at the edge of my bunkbed when I heard this alarming question. From what I could gather on Sundays, God was a source of good, the ultimate defender to all those who called on him in their battles. His love was powerful, so much so that it could raise the dead to living, breathing life. He despised evil and relational discord. Except now, sitting in the middle of this treacherous war with no reply to my desperate pleading, my understanding began to change. The more I thought about it, the more alone I felt in my circumstances. I started to doubt that God could really care for me from such a distant and deaf position.

Despair and anger settled instantly into my heart, an unexpected intrusion of feelings I had not yet been acquainted with. I distinctly remember feeling my entire being tear in two, as if I had been blindsided by a sword in the hands of an unknown opponent. My heart split as the laceration caused two halves to be left linked by mere strands, which seemed only to exist for the purpose of honoring the severed connection. It was an unforgettable feeling. God could change things, yet he didn't. I felt abandoned and began to question how God could be trusted for his supposed goodness. If he was so great, how could he ignore the prayers of a child like me?

I never told anyone about that night or about that part of my life. I never told anyone how discouraging it was to know that there was something out there with the ability to help, sitting idle. God's presence started to feel more cruel than good. I cried myself to sleep, trying to figure out what I was doing or saying that was so wrong in my prayers for God to ignore me the way he was. My concept of trust was on life support before I even turned ten. I loved my parents deeply, but I also deeply despised the hopelessness they projected. My parents worked hard to provide a nice home for us, healthy food on the table, and the best clothes they could afford. Call me ungrateful, but I just knew there was more to life than shelter, food, and clothes.

Necessities to physical life often confused with life's purpose, where people become a secondary means to the end. It was difficult for me to appreciate home when it rarely felt safe, or clothes and food when the price tags on each so easily stirred hours of discord. I was desperate for peace, stability, and nurturing encouragement, the absence of which left me voiceless, invalidated, and lost.

With peace and gratitude,
Chole

Public Enemies

Dear Addie, may this note find you well.

As children, we are not taught about the dangers of deceitful distortions of truth or the subtle traps cleverly set to oppress our pure desires. The threats that more commonly warranted parental caution were those such as talking to strangers, crossing the busy street, or defending ourselves against schoolyard bullies. It irritated me to my core that we as humans essentially train each other to defend ourselves against one another, moreover within the trivial confines of what we can see. We attempt unity on fallible bases, and when that doesn't work, we resort to making rules that lawfully demand we treat one another well. We educate in an effort to prevent ourselves from physical harm, but those lessons negate preparedness for when we face the real public enemies. If they too were exposed with cautionary notice, we would be taught to know their ways and be on the lookout for them every moment of every single day. We would be so intimately aware of their presence that we could call them out by name: arrogance, greed, jealousy, lust, laziness, anger, and gluttony. And instead of a punch, we would be trained to triumph over them with a Word. Nevertheless, daily life generally lends little concern for the influence these enemies have on us.

The influence was clear to me; what wasn't was love's inability to have the same. After each emotional explosion at home, life would hurry on as if nothing had even happened. The debris was cleaned up, leaving no trace of dismantling, further permitting the manipulation of unapologetic defendants to desensitize the pain. It was the type of love often described in song lyrics as a maddening push and pull, where hatred for the other is just a buildup to passionate reconciliation. Where jealousy and drama show how much you care, and blame acts as the Band-Aid over stubborn wounds. Toxic avoidance of accountability so persuasive it lent itself to be curing truth. Truth that ultimately attempted to declare that this was unconditional love, love that bears all things while silently accepting infraction. Love that always remains together, despite the consistent dishonoring of others. Love that claims to be selfless through impatience and anger. Love that respects the boundary walls of the home, where transgression could be hidden in the form of gag orders and counterfeit smiles. Something never felt completely right about love associated in these ways, as if lives permeated by selfish acts, completely absent of responsibility, were supposed to be where grace abounded. I observed this version of love to be normal; however, I could not accept it as such. It was catastrophic confusion.

Believing God cared was becoming more debatable as I became more intimately acquainted with reality in the world. Illness, financial struggle, addiction, and relationship conflict were more prevalent in my life than traditional adolescent problems. Worrying about who to go to the dance with or who the in crowd consisted of seemed utterly trivial compared to the weight my mom-mom felt making a purchase with food stamps for the first time. While my peers wandered the sidelines of the football field on Friday nights, I roamed the aisles at the grocery store. My mom-mom, my mother's mother, was a tiny woman with blonde hair and blue eyes and a smile as big as her face could fit. On the surface, you would never know her world as she knew it was unraveling around her. My pop-pop, my mother's father, achieved great financial wealth as a small-business owner prior to his diagnosis. He owned an electronic repair shop at the height of the art of fixing things. After years of witnessing him drift away without reason, he was diagnosed with Alzheimer's disease. The burden of caring for someone with an erratic diagnosis was heavy enough without the fact that he was persuaded to donate their life savings to a prosperity gospel church while out of his sound mind. He was a Bible-believing evangelist, deceived in a vulnerable state by the very thing he loved the most.

His financial fumble propelled him and my mom-mom into poverty. Security in the form of money had vaporized, and certainty in daily routines and self-dependence had collapsed. The way my mom-mom responded to these life trials captivated me in my state of questioning about God. Don't get me wrong; she fought like the best of them. She came from a time when men handled the finances, so when her trust in that confident reliance betrayed her, she demanded answers. The arguing was endless, as nobody knew how to navigate the uncharted territory of interdependence laid before them. I was puzzled by the guilt-soaked actions and bitter words bearing with these burdens had plagued upon associated hearts.

When she and I were alone, she spoke differently about it all. Where one might expect to hear continual speech of devastation, she proclaimed hope. In the face of the unknown, she trusted that Jesus would always provide, furthermore making sure that everyone she encountered knew his name for that reason. Friday-night grocery shopping took three hours on average, mainly because she talked to everyone she saw. When I heard her start to talk about Jesus, I would continue to the next aisle, agitated beyond words, wondering why she had to prolong this simple task. That was just it though: it wasn't a task to her. She loved people and saw every encounter as an opportunity to love, even if all she had left to give were words of encouragement. She was without the luxuries and comforts she was used to, yet she was content having everything she needed. As we continued to shop, she would tell me stories about the big house and pool they used to have and about the trips she would take on the trolley into Philadelphia to have custom shoes and dresses made for my mother as a child.

At the time, I couldn't comprehend what it would be like to go from being able to buy whatever you wanted to having to calculate each purchase to the penny. The only time I saw her display any sort of discomfort toward her circumstances was when it came time to check out. She understood the fact that her only access to food now was via a government-issued card, yet ultimately, she could not bear to use it. The mere act of retrieving it from her purse caused her to become tense and bewildered. I remember ignorantly interrogating her to understand why it was such a big deal, to which she responded speechless with an agonizing expression. Overcome with remorse, I decided from that point on to personally and privately handle checkout. I would slip the card from inside her purse a few aisles before approaching the cashier, then discreetly swipe it while she wasn't looking, so by the time the food was bagged, the anxiety of payment was nonexistent. This routine lasted for years, and we became close confidants.

On Saturdays, I would help her with chores and caring for my pop-pop. As soon as I arrived, Mom-Mom would make tea and tell me stories about her life. She loved the smell of coffee but despised the taste, so teatime became an added element of our regimen. After settling in, I would walk my pop-pop upstairs to shave his face and trim his nails. Some days, he complied; others, he resisted. The hardest days were when he was absent, as wandering was just one of the phases of his dreaded illness. Waiting in suspense during these search parties added to the heaping pile of anxiety mounting within my family. Saturday afternoons, we would transition to my great-aunt Cassie's house, my mom-mom's sister, who also needed help, as a heart condition rendered living alone very difficult for her. She resided alone because her husband had abandoned her. As I cleaned and cooked, I would listen to her life in stories: a heart once filled with fun and happiness as a young woman had been hurt by broken love and mangled promises. Some days, she acquired so much fluid in her legs that she would develop sores that served as small drains for the excess water. I would unwrap her legs, gently clean her wounds, and medicate and wrap them again. Everyone would talk of how I should go to nursing school for the care I administered all around. I just saw it as the way of life, serving one another so no one was in need, without reimbursement for it. Acceptable restitution came in the form of dimes and quarters so that I could run to the convenience store across the street for a snack.

Sundays were my favorite of all days growing up. There was something about the day, something noticeably different about it, as if peace and hope had authority over the air. My parents made it a point that we heard the Gospel on Sunday morning and ate with my grandmom and grandpop, my father's parents, on Sunday night. It was one of the two places I felt like a true kid in my life. The other was in my backyard at home during the summer, playing endless games of Wiffle ball and home run derby. At my grandparents', I was free to play outside with my siblings, without responsibility or obligation other than to raid the shed for the latest outdoor toys. My grandfather was also a successful businessman, owning a small grocery store in the city. They lived off of a golf course with a yard filled with carpet-like grass outlined with fruit trees. The picturesque perfectness of that house equated to an undercurrent of peace for me. It wasn't hard to associate money with security when you arrived there, especially given the stark contrast to the eight-by-eight patch of lawn enclosed by a chain-link fence at my mom-mom's recent residence. The things at these homes, however, didn't leave as deep an impression as the limitations they represented did.

Certain areas of the house were off-limits to kids at my grandparents', like the second-floor sitting room and the upstairs bathroom, in effort to preserve the immaculate nature of the valuables in those spaces. I appreciated how hard my grandmother worked to keep an orderly house yet couldn't escape how unloved I felt sitting on the floor in front of a perfectly fine couch reserved for mature consumers, or what made me so unclean to be restricted to refreshing myself in the utility room sink. My mom-mom loved being a homemaker as well and preserved her couch with a plastic covering because she knew she couldn't afford another one should a spill or accident occur. Anyone could sit, just as long as they were sitting on plastic. All of it made me wonder what was cared about most, the comfort of the person or preservation of the material. Mom-mom also loved to garden, and while her patch of lawn was the most beautiful of all in her row, my heart petitioned to know why these joys in life were given to some and taken from others.

After hours of playing outside and picking apples for dessert pie, we washed up for pasta dinner. Food was important in my family; there was something sacred about sharing it together, in particular. Sharing in the tastes, in the recipe criticism, and in the prayer of thanks before eating. Ironically, the prayer, which I expected to bring us closer together, was the dividing factor. My grandparents said a Catholic prayer that I could never seem to memorize, followed by making the sign of the cross, which we also did not do. Dishonoring those obligated words and notions lent to judgmental eyes that said our Protestant practice of faith was a lesser version than that of Catholicism. Nevertheless, mealtime was still something to be revered and savored, never disregarded or rushed, homemade and never from a box. What to eat for dinner was often the topic of discussion before breakfast, and leftovers did not go to waste. I was the only kid at lunch with breaded eggplant as a side to chicken cutlet sandwiches. Even during the week, nothing came in the way of sharing dinner together. If my father was on night shift, he would call precisely at the dinner hour to speak to each of us, ask us about our day, and tell us what he was eating at work while we ate at home. Then we would individually exchange our nightly salutation: "Good night. God bless you. I love you." Those exchanges were what I clung to for hope, hope that there was love somewhere buried beneath the actions that may have disproved otherwise.

Regrettably, dysfunction didn't take the day off on Sunday, as the ride home always guaranteed an argument of sorts. Controversy perpetually stemmed from an invisible provocateur, spurring the same conundrum of conflicting identities. Despite how many times the words "I love you" were spoken, toxic traits of insecurity, disrespect, and control still caused joy to be momentary, peace to be circumstantial, and acceptance to be conditional.

With peace and gratitude,
Chole

How to Hide

Dear Addie, may this note find you well.

Those Sunday drives home, along with every single family car ride in general, were accompanied by an alcohol-infused argument and forcibly submitted passengers. I physically complied because I had no choice. Refusing to get in the car as I got older only made it worse and drew unwanted attention to what everyone was trying to deny. An indisputable seed of angst was sprouting in my heart. I hated my father for being so inconsiderate of our lives. He defended his recklessness and arrogance as a victim of false accusation, criticizing us for not trusting his ability to defy his inebriated state. I hated my mother for being powerless over my father. She would reach her arm back past her seat to rub our legs as we shook and cried, knowing her children were in danger yet helpless from being able to protect us from it. What troubled my mind the most through those experiences was the fact that she would defend him to us. She would actually take up for him by trying to convince us that he was just tired from working so hard—as if we didn't have eyes of our own to see his unleashed anger in action when he got into fist fights, ears to hear the slurred insults and blaring music on school nights, or hearts to feel the insidious hurt. I have to believe that she didn't know she was invalidating my response to abuse by telling me to keep my mouth shut and not defend myself. When I did speak out, which was often, I was told how much I disobeyed the commandment to honor my mother and father. All that did was pile guilt on to an already confused young mind, leaving me to wonder what role honor and love played here. I didn't know how to honor my parents, especially if it meant standing passive in the face of blatant mistreatment.

There was not one adult in my life who didn't undermine my understanding of this behavior to be harmful. Family and friends enabled the problem by continuing to serve him while taking laughing pleasure in the drunken jokes, before, of course, silently watching us leave every gathering, knowing there was a risk we might not make it home. Love in its true form of selfless surrender of personal desires for the well-being of another, humble confrontation, and vulnerable accountability were persistently neglected. People were more comfortable empowering a problem in an effort to keep the peace than they were courageously standing up for children who could not speak for themselves. That led me to despise how often everyone said, "I love you." Absent of loving action, they were just empty words to me. How can you love someone while displaying more regard for your own interests and desires than that of the one you say you love? How can one truly love another if the meaning of the word is founded in their own interpretation of the definition? How could we all claim to follow Jesus on Sunday and yet live each day in outright opposition to his ways? These varying degrees of love associated with belief in the same God generated a profound insurrection in my heart. Perhaps most discouraging of all was the fact that love, all powerful as it was, could be so easily corrupted.

Hate was a strong word that surfaced all too frequently in my vocabulary back then. I was fiercely passionate toward what I didn't like and arbitrarily docile to what I did. It was difficult to find peace between the extremes. When life was good, it was great; however, when things were bad, they were absolutely awful. A delightful meal shared by people who seemingly adored one another would turn into the deepest war of words if anyone requested my father ease off drinking. Rotten, soul-provoking angst would spew if said person to speak up was me, which was, again, most of the time. Being instinctively forced to learn how to mindfully walk on eggshells was as effective as physically trying to teach a baby how to walk unassisted for the first time on a water mattress. The fact that our relational foundation had the ability to collapse in an instant made me wonder what foundation it was built on. It also prompted me to want to know what foundation was required to prevent the architectural compromise. The ceaseless roller coaster of emotions fostered a connectedness between love and hate that took root in an all too natural of way.

Despite the intense push and pull, I held strong to hope in a form of love that was powerful enough to invoke authentic change. Life-changing love that was tangible, consistent, and simultaneously unyielding. That happened to be the exact opposite of what I was learning the definition of the word to be. The notion of loving others the way Jesus loves us seemed to be as revolutionary an idea in 1999 as it was when he walked the earth. High school, a.k.a. preparation for the real world, was through my eyes a me-first cultivating culture. What mattered most was exploring *my* interests, *my* happiness, and *my* dreams. Discerning how *I* would spend *my* time on this earth to make it as successful as possible for *me*. I found that to be an utterly useless endeavor, not to mention dangerous. The lack of focus on how my decisions aligned with God's ways, or other humans for that matter, made discerning right from wrong even more confusing for me than it already was.

It was no secret that I struggled to respect authority, particularly those with a "do as I say, not as I do" type of force. It provoked an unsettling level of anger within me that ultimately manifested as rebellion. Somewhere between second and third grade, I developed a self-defined social justice movement. One occasion I remember vividly, during art class, I persuaded my classmates to use their poster-board to make picket signs. I instructed them to fold the posters and bring them out to recess. When our teachers came out to get us, I initiated a chant protesting the return to the classroom. Most kids crumbled and abandoned the cause when discipline was proposed. The ones who stuck with me were warned to avoid me and my poor influence. As for me, I was sent straight to the principal's office. I averaged a few hours a week in that office and had no problem serving time in an air-conditioned environment—hardly an honorable disciplinary action was my train of thought.

The charm of being a soldier for social justice at school wore thin as instability at home heightened. It was isolating, being in trouble at home and at school all of the time. Midway through grade school, I shifted focus toward trying to be good, paying more attention to learning, and seeking encouraging activities. I achieved scholar athlete, most notably for being captain of the volleyball team against the odds of the height norm for the sport. I mastered a high serve with a heavy drop that most opponents found impossible to return. I had never played volleyball before that year, so it was a new feeling, being good at something. The title of captain didn't matter; I was fixated on the fact that I could do something that I enjoyed that didn't get me into trouble. The life span of that feeling would be brief though, thanks to a demeaning, sarcastic coach. The volleyball coach at our school was an overweight man who instructed us from a chair on the sidelines. His limitations didn't bother me; just his mouth did. He would call me names each time I made a mistake, then mock me when plays weren't perfect enough. At one of the last games in the season, he shouted obscenities at me when I refused to smile. He pulled me from the game and said I was benched until my attitude changed. I asked what smiling had to do with playing the game, to which he grabbed my face and replied that I was the captain and responsible for playing with a positive attitude in addition to performing well. While there was some merit in the critique, all I could think about was how his failure to coach was my fault. I was angry at myself for allowing his foul demeanor to influence mine. His liberal use of derogatory terms toward me was extremely demotivating as I tried my hardest to perfect a game I had never played before. I didn't know how to work with that, so I took off my jersey, threw it at him, and walked out. To my dismay, we were at an away game, and I didn't have previous permission to ride home with my mom, so I had no choice but to eat crow and wait out the rest of the evening. It's sad to be writing this to you, realizing how much anger I carried even back then. And yet there's a part of me that wonders why more people aren't angry about the hardness that callouses the output of our hearts.

I continued trying new sports, but the struggle to fit into the associated crowd deflated my interest. It was a defeating concession because I enjoyed playing so much. In addition to a degrading instructor, the dominating emphasis on the social association with sports stole the innocence away from it for me. I'd be lying if I said I didn't slightly desire to be included in the jock clique; however, the weekend house parties where otherwise healthy athletes sought drugs, alcohol, and sex for fun was enough of a turnoff to keep my distance. I had witnessed enough destruction from drugs and alcohol in my life; I could not comprehend consuming either myself, let alone for pleasure. The dichotomy was an official introduction to the reality of cliques. On the outside, it was enticing to be part of a group of people who shared the same interests and actively shared life together. The sisterlike bond my female classmates shared fascinated me, but I could never trust anyone to get so close.

I think subconsciously I knew it was impossible to make friends without getting so close, so I worked on perfecting the art of social survival. That essentially meant achieving a delicate balance between being adequately liked and sufficiently invisible. Finding this footing was especially crucial when it came to the topic of dating. Dating always felt much more like an obligation than it ever did a delight. When I was seven years old, I saw an episode of *Full House* where Rebecca gave birth to twins. I remember running hysterical into the kitchen to tell my mother that I was never going to get married or have babies. She giggled and said, "Okay, you don't have to." It was humorous to her when I was seven, then devastatingly concerning that I held the same position when I was seventeen. In concession, and in effort to avoid being a disappointment, I chose to pretend, a seemingly small sacrifice in the name of politeness. Dating was just unquestionably agonizing for me; I couldn't wait for it to be over before it had even begun. If only politeness equated to some level of pleasure. I couldn't help but perceive the whole notion of it to be an awkward human hunt. And every date was the same, a venture to some local chain restaurant where the main course consisted of forced conversation with a side of awkward silence.

The colossal lack of authenticity paired with overt scales of desperate sensuality, where eyes would otherwise be exposed for their self-serving purpose, left me feeling like a species of prey. Words from scripture that emphasized the complementary companionship and mutual respect between men and women reeled around in my head as I participated in a much more clumsy, disappointing dance. What real interest could any one of these guys have in me without knowing a single fact about my life besides my name, their idea of me, and what I looked like? All this effort—and for what, to get a kiss from a girl? My God, have mercy on the desperation. It was the most dreadful way I could think of to spend precious time. Add to it the pressure to dress a certain way, speak the right words, or even consume certain foods in order to be deemed desirable, and it was downright demoralizing. I couldn't be bothered; my mind was fixated on obtaining the requirements for a high school diploma so that I could move on.

I craved independence in such a bad way that I found no advantage to having a significant other. I spent my entire adolescence cleaning up men's failures to be providers and cherishers of their wives' well-being. They boasted about how they earned the money, as if that also earned them the right to cheapen women for their role as homemaker and mother. It pained my heart to watch the women in my life work so hard, only to have a paycheck held over them in place of a considerate life cohort and emotional security. I interpreted men's desire for women to be one of service with self-righteous, unequal respect in return. I despised that idea, along with their utter failures to be compassionate, selfless, loving partners in an already turbulent world. The idea of willingly entering that vicious cycle felt like a burden; there was nothing they could offer that I could not set out to achieve on my own. I was also vehemently tired of being a victim of my father's poisonous choices, which didn't aid in the enticement to date one bit. My thinking was countercultural and a metaphorical punch to my family's expectations for my life.

I felt misunderstood and misplaced most, if not all, of the time. There was a fire raging within me to know God's intention for humanity, to wholeheartedly understand the gap between his purpose and our chosen ones. I wanted the chance to make my own decisions and to live according to God's ways more than I wanted anything else. And yet the one thing I innately treasured most was also the one area I couldn't find a single soul to remotely share an interest. It seemed like the things I despised most, like parties and dating, were all anyone wanted to talk about—even at church. High school held the promise of transformative growth yet under delivered with a superficial focus on social status. This ironically led to my most memorable lesson: how to hide.

With peace and gratitude,
Chole

Free Will

Dear Addie, may this note find you well.

I have now told you more about my life in a few letters than I ever did in the time I knew you. In fact, I've never talked about my life in such depth with another human being up to this point. Much of what I have shared has been buried beneath the surface of my thoughts and actions, rarely if at all expressed in any form of relational communication. I think it would hurt my family to read some of the things I've written, as if I'm betraying them by divulging these secrets that everyone knows and nobody speaks about. I think they would also see it as an unfair balance, a one-sided perspective of the bad times without equal attention to the good. And there was a lot of good; I think we just differed on the definition of the word.

My father dropped out of college after he met my mother so that he could start working to be a good provider. From what I gathered, his parents were not happy with that decision. He took a dredging job with an oil company, working late nights and early mornings. That was the beginning of a career in oil refining. He worked twelve-hour rotating shifts between day and night, an extremely taxing schedule both physically and mentally, in exchange for one of the best monetary job trajectories without a college degree. He bought a home and a car and supported his wife without any assistance from his parents, or anyone, for that matter. When we were born, he always said he was motivated to work in unfavorable conditions so that his wife would not have to work and so that his kids were well taken care of. Before he left the house, he said he would look around and remind himself of how what he was about to do provided well for his family; that's what got him through the day. His work didn't end when his shift did. He would come home and mow the lawn or take on home repairs. He was always working for his family, as well as anyone else in need, whether it was neighbors or friends.

My mother also worked very hard to keep a clean and orderly home for us while caring for her parents. She made sure we were safely driven to and from school, ate healthy meals, were involved in extracurricular activities, completed all of our holy sacraments, and had the best of everything, even if it was at the expense of her own needs. Despite financial limitations, the Christmas tree always overflowed with gifts, Easter baskets had treats regardless of age, and birthdays were always celebrated on the day. Their love touched people throughout our lives. Anyone experiencing hard times always felt safe coming to our house because they knew my parents would receive them without judgment. They would get a warm meal, a drink, maybe a few bucks, a compassionate ear, and a sendoff in love. This was the only perspective I portrayed of my family outside of our home. I suppressed the damaging aspects deep enough to where I even had myself convinced they had no effect on me. I was taught at an early age that the good was all that needed to be displayed. The bad was private and sacred, nobody else's business. In that scenario, there are not many options other than to bottle it up.

The space between the good and bad was where I found myself stuck. I couldn't comprehend how good intentions could be carried out with such passionate anger, impatient obligation, and vile frustration. My father worked hard, yet he worked angry. My mother worked hard, yet she worked bitterly. Neither of them ever seemed to operate with a true sense of joy or peace. Yes, there were moments of laughter and happy occasions—each, however, fleeting as they were. This was life, so I was told, according to generations of wisdom. You're born into circumstances out of your control, life becoming the sum of what happens to you and what you make of that. Somewhere in between, you make conscious choices toward happiness, like marriage, children, hobbies, and careers. Perhaps that's what had everyone so up in arms about my stance toward these things. I wanted to take a more proactive approach to life; I didn't want it to be something that just happened. I wanted more say than that. I didn't see marriage as the sole love generator, nor building a family as the only path toward fulfilling happiness.

Hiding was emotionally safer than being true to myself; however, pretending to be someone I wasn't was effectively a whole other challenge. Cultural pressures alone made it difficult to choose the right persona to display. Furthermore, I didn't know how to separate who I was from whose I was, and I belonged to my family. I was a daughter, a granddaughter, a niece, a sister, and a cousin. My allegiance, my time, and my obligation to serve in this world were first and foremost to my people. Therefore, my own identity at its core was rooted in the sum of the lives of those who comprised my immediate and extended family unit. The conflicting emotions of being both proud and ashamed of who this meant I was made it impossible to believe I could be accepted for my true self. If I had told anyone about the dysfunction and brokenness that plagued our lives, I risked being known for demotivating hardship, crippling flaws, and a dismembered adaptation of love. That wasn't all. I was a parent-dishonoring, rule-resistant, rage-filled young woman. Confessing that meant giving other people the power to criticize, judge, and reject me. The emphasis on social status in this world demanded I protect myself, with crushing pressure to achieve acceptance by deceiving reality, so I painted a new family portrait, one where I was the perfect churchgoing, family-serving, studious middle child in a large, vivacious family. The key was to never let anyone get close enough to see that the picture was actually counterfeit.

Sustaining such a safe distance required me to restrict admission into my life, except for a purpose. The purpose of accepting a guy into my life was only to keep my family's disappointment in me at bay. As much as I struggled in my family dynamic, I still loved them deeply and even more so desired their acceptance. I knew what they had in mind for my life, so I applied specific criteria to the guys I dated: athletic, older, and of Eastern European decent. I baited with a steady level of flirting to maintain the guy's attention long enough to make the engagement seem authentic. I released him once the realization of zero chance of intimacy sparked disinterest. I dated a lot in high school, all good guys given my deceit. The game of chase provided exactly what I needed. Since I owned the prize, I also held control over when the game needed to expire. It was a predictable and reliable system. I carried out the same scheme with girl friends, acting as if I actually cared about boy drama, long hairstyles, and manicured nails. I would get the insiders' scoop on what guys they were trying to impress, then make them my targets. Somehow, I landed on the homecoming court senior year and, without trying too hard, had two escorts for prom. I adored the captain of the hockey team as a friend, which made it difficult to string him along half of the year to secure the date. The other came out of nowhere—tall, handsome, funny, blond hair with blue eyes. He would make surprise visits to my house and play basketball with me and my little brother. He instantly won the adoration of my family, so I allowed the entry into my personal sphere for the time being. It was hard to tell him no when he asked me to the prom, especially when he left his longtime girlfriend for just a chance to hang out with me by the end of the event. My family thought I was attractive and popular, girls didn't want to be close friends, and guys started to notice I was the ultimate chase. All bought into the deception; I couldn't have planned it better if I tried.

With a social life being such a big part of our formative years, how can it be a shock that this is what most of us plot and plan our lives around? The desire for acceptance and the fear of rejection is the chasm we are literally raised in. Without the proper weapons, and without a greater focus than ourselves, survival is really the only logical mentality. I suppose that is where the fight-or-flight mentality is born. It speaks with clarity to our emotions, particularly in moments of need and want, defying patient and long-suffering endurance by enticing with instant gratification. Flight was my reaction of choice, especially once I obtained the ability to drive. Before, when my father would tell me to get out, I would leave in fury and walk to my mom-mom's. Having the ability to go farther than my own two feet could take me was a whole new level of freedom in those instances. I would drive for hours through quiet neighborhoods, dreaming of achieving that peace, dreaming of owning my own home, where there was no fighting or disparagement. Peace for me resided there, in the absence of conflict. It also resided in a place of independence, in the absence of being someone's obligation. If I dreaded anything more than dating, it was the idea of depending on another person to provide for me.

A new fight was brewing within my heart. I had exhausted myself in prayer to the tune of no reply. My circumstances showed no signs of changing, as I had begged for almost ten years by then. That familiar voice from my youth was back: *if they really loved you, they would change.* I heard it each time I was in conflict with someone in my family unit. I figured there to be some sense of truth in that statement, given I was searching for life-altering love and peace. I told God that I didn't know how to wait on him anymore, reminding him of how long I had been asking for help. With still no reply, I saw no other choice than to turn my dependence fully to myself to get out of my circumstances. I was the only one who saw value in obtaining peace and cultivating love; therefore, it was on me to make it happen. As hard as I tried to rely on God, I could not see any other way than to make it on my own.

With peace and gratitude,
Chole

Dreams

Dear Addie, may this note find you well.

When I was about eight years old, I had visions of Jesus coming down from heaven, riding on clouds with angels and trumpets. The dreams were so vivid I would wake up wanting to go back to sleep to see more. I never told anyone about the dreams because I was afraid of being made fun of. My relationship with Jesus was my most cherished possession; I could handle being ridiculed for other parts of my life, just not this one. Some kids have certain toys or keepsakes they adore. I had Jesus. It wasn't a tangible item to keep in a secret chest; it was a virtuous conviction hidden in my heart. I do not recall hearing or reading any scripture as a kid that would have fed the visions I saw; it wasn't until later in life I was able to pair the dreams with words written thousands of years before my existence. My fascination with Jesus wasn't spurred so much by that vision as it was rooted in a promise he held that nothing else in the world did. He promised to change things, to take what was old and restore it to new. Arguing, poverty, bitterness, anger, injustice, and rejection were all getting old to me. I was hungry to find out exactly what Jesus meant in his promise to change all of these things, and I further thought that belief in him was enough to bring about such changes. It was a theory I might have trusted if there had been even the slightest reflection of renewal in anyone around me. Maybe people really didn't change, as the saying went. I still wanted to know how and when Jesus would go about making things new. I looked for signs of this in the people around me, particularly those who said they believed in Jesus. The kids at church formed cliques just like at school; nothing new there. I observed the adults in the pews to see how they responded to the Good News being preached to them. I wondered how good this news could be if people were falling asleep listening to it and reacting with monotone hallelujahs. As if that wasn't uninspiring enough, listening to the gossip at coffee hour was downright depressing.

I knew there was more to the message and that church was supposed to be a good place. Something was overtly missing though. While my heart maintained an eager burning to know what that *more* was, my mind said it was time to face reality, which required more action and less conceptual notion. College was not an automatic next step in my family. It was assumed that men worked and earned money, while women had children and became homemakers. The fact that I even wanted to go to college was a fight. It was a decision that impacted my life, the first one I felt like I could actually make for myself, yet here I was again with everyone who said they loved me standing in the way. The women in my life tried to convince me to find a nice man and get married so that he could earn the money. My grandfather and father showed zero confidence in my ability to succeed and instead reminded me of how hard it was for women to get good jobs, even with a college degree. Little did they know they were throwing fuel on my fire. Their disbelief in my ability was enough for me to now have to prove them wrong and do so by exceeding their levels of financial success.

I applied to two schools, Drexel University and Neumann University. I knew where I wanted to go, and if I'd had it my way, I would have only applied to Drexel. Neumann was my mother's choice, as it was closer to home in the suburbs. Drexel was the clear winner for me, as it promised a professional focus, city experience, and the opportunity to work while learning through the cooperative program. The ability to work meant I could prove myself in a manner other than grades. I was a poor test taker from the time I entered school in kindergarten; an aptitude test going into first grade proved as much. Book smarts were never my strong suit, nor were books how I learned well. I was an experiential, hands-on learner. The only way I was going to make my plans come to fruition was by playing to my strengths. My will back then was like an immovable force: once I made up my mind about something, there was no stopping me.

I received a letter from Drexel shortly after applying stating their conditional acceptance of my application. The condition was based on attending and passing their summer boot camp program prior to fall enrollment. I had a 3.8 GPA, a few academic awards, and a handful of sports acknowledgments on my high school résumé. Since serving my family on nights and weekends didn't count as volunteer work, there was a clear gap in what I didn't know to be a requirement for college entry. Boot camp consisted of a twelve-hour daily residential curriculum for eight weeks, with two one-hour breaks per day for meals, and weekends off. We were told at the offset that only 60 percent tended to make it to the end. I was going to make it, whatever it took. The coursework was challenging; however, it didn't seem like that was what they were looking at. They were looking to see if we could handle the fast, intense pace of Drexel's trimester system. The other aspect they were looking to introduce was diversity, as each of us was paired with a roommate of the opposite ethnicity from ourselves. I enjoyed that aspect most of all. It dispelled the various racial innuendos I had grown up with, including the ones aimed at me personally. I was bullied through all of middle school for being darker skinned than other kids, especially for being darker than my own siblings. Kids would throw spitballs at me on the bus during class trips, calling me a wetback and Oreo. God made my skin color the way it was; if they had an issue with it, they could take it up with him, as far as I was concerned. That always seemed like such a lame and trivial way to differentiate people, as if we even have the power to claim ownership in any aspect of how we are made. How much more irreverent of God can we be, alleging one to be better than another as if we ourselves are the creators? Unreal.

I made it to the end of that summer, as predicted with a group of folks 40 percent less than when we started. It felt like a great accomplishment and a much better way to have spent the summer than how I heard some of my high school acquaintances had, drinking at the shore and such. I had my momentary taste of that just prior to boot camp. To each his own; I just happened to find it lifeless. I ended high school with one good friend, Lily. I didn't feel like I had to change who I was to be around her and genuinely enjoyed her company. I hung out at her house a lot that year, even though there were make-out sessions and drinking; I tolerated it because I trusted her judgment. She invited me down the shore to spend senior week with her and her friends, and since I hadn't gone on many social outings with groups during school, I decided to go. It would be the only week I had off between high school ending and boot camp beginning, so I had to make it count. It was fun at first, hanging out on the beach with no schedule or parents telling you where to go or what to do. As the week went on, though, it got to be exhausting and boring. Beach during the day and drinking games at night. One other boy and I were the only single people there, which should have been the only red flag I needed to decline. It was clearly a setup, and he was obnoxiously persistent. If I had driven myself there, I probably would have lasted two days max. By the last night, I wanted away from that scene so badly I was looking forward to boot camp.

Lily's older sister Lucy and her friend Emma showed up that last night to pick up the alcohol. They were the transporters, given the rest of us were underage. Lily was just about finished cleaning the house in preparation for our checkout the following day when Lucy asked if I wanted to stay behind to hang out instead of going to dinner with my friends. Something told me it would be much more fun hanging with them than being coupled up with this annoying guy everyone had been trying to match me with all week. Prior to that, I had been thinking about how my decision to be there made me realize that finding friends who didn't drink and who also wanted to learn about Jesus was a seemingly impossible task. I was disappointed in myself for compromising my disdain for alcohol in an effort to fit in. After everyone left for dinner, Lucy turned on some music and started making drinks. I wasn't sure what to expect and certainly hadn't envisioned more drinking being in the equation. I thought I would help them pack up, talk, and such. An hour later, I found myself covered in daiquiri, dancing on the previously cleaned kitchen table. Turned out Lucy was like a comedian on steroids. Amid the laughter, we realized we had made a huge mess in the kitchen and didn't have time to clean it up before everyone started arriving back home. We darted out the back door and ran straight for the beach.

There was a moment in time that night where I felt unconditionally free. There was no pressure to impress, conversation was easy and entertaining, and I felt genuinely welcomed in Lucy's company. We walked the shoreline for what seemed like hours, until the moon was the only light left on. We climbed up onto a lifeguard stand so that we could sit and watch the waves in the quietude. Staring out at the sea's horizon, I could feel a difference in the world. I was completely myself, and there was no criticism or disappointment in return, just a palpable rush of peace and happiness. I turned toward Lucy to share my thoughts and found her leaning in to kiss me. I had no idea what she was doing; however, before I could even process it, a police officer shined a flashlight on us, demanding we get down from the lifeguard stand.

We ran away, giggling uncontrollably. By the time we got back to the house, everyone was sleeping. I went to bed encapsulated by the new feelings, still obliviously unaware of the meaning behind the attempted kiss. It wasn't until the morning that I knew something might have been wrong about it. Nobody was talking to me, including Lily. It was a long and silent ride home. I apologized for making the mess in the kitchen and for not cleaning it up before checkout, figuring that was the reason she was angry with me. She dropped me off without reply, and we never spoke again, to this day. I would come to find that she hated her sister's sexuality and assumed I was now the same for spending the night with her. I would like to admit that it hurt, and it did for a short time. Nonetheless, I felt more like my true self with Lucy in one night than I had all year with Lily and her friends. It made me wonder why I cared so much about what other people thought of me, why I allowed people's perceptions to dictate my reality, limit my choices, and shape some duller version of myself. I didn't have to morph into those church people in order to love God, nor did I have to conform to my family's expectations for my life in order to cultivate peace and happiness. That night, running carefree under God's starlit sky along his vast sea, left a deep impression on me: peace and happiness were real. I just had to figure out how to obtain them.

With peace and gratitude,
Chole

Instinct

Dear Addie, may this note find you well.

My first trimester in college began with a lot of drive and excitement, quickly clouded by the declining health of my pop-pop. After a series of mini-strokes, the treatment he needed exceeded my mom-mom's abilities to care for him at home. His rehabilitation center happened to be the second stop off the train I took into the city for school every day. I would get on with full intent to go to class, until I pictured him lying there alone in his room. It wasn't like he didn't have visitors; the rest of my family would come to be with him in the late afternoon and evenings. The mornings, however, he was alone, and I didn't think it was good for anyone in such a circumstance to be alone like that. I skipped half of my first classes jumping off at that second stop. I'm not quite sure he knew who I was or that I was even there, since the dementia had taken over his mind by that point. Still, I thought a familiar presence in the room would be of comfort to him. I tried using the time to study since he slept most of the time, but I often got distracted by the sounds of pain and distress echoing in the halls from the other patients. Pop-pop didn't appear to be in any pain; the most visible suffering was when he aspirated food. I remember being in those meetings with the nurses, my mom-mom, and my mom, making decisions for his life. The decision to permit food through a tube when he lost the muscular function to swallow, the decision to resuscitate or not if he lost brain function. Alone in there with him, I would rarely end up studying. Instead, I would find myself staring at him, contemplating the purpose of my selfish endeavors as I watched his life come to an end. What was it all for? The toil and trials that were once all-consuming problems were now meaningless in the face of death. I was too young to get to know him before he got sick; all I knew was from the time I spent caring for him and the stories my mom-mom told me about his life. Yet there I was, alongside my mom and my aunt, when he took his last breath. I was there when my mom-mom walked in to embrace his lifeless body after she had left only moments before to shower and rest. She said he'd waited for her to go to spare her the agony of the moment. I skipped most of my second trimester those following months by never even getting on the train. The train station was just across the street from where my mom-mom lived. I would tell myself that I would just skip the first class so that I could give her a little company, but it never worked out that way. We would sit for hours, sipping tea and talking, or if the weather was nice, we would garden.

I was forced back into focus by the third trimester after receiving a notice of academic probation for missing so much class time. My heart was heavily distracted, watching my mother grieve the loss of her father and my mom-mom the loss of her husband of fifty years. The world doesn't offer much time for bereavement though; it rushes on as if heartache is a trivial personal problem. Work and responsibilities don't pause. Bills are still due. I didn't appreciate the hard line between what I could be doing to bear with a widow in mourning and what I had to do, which was school. Spending enough time at my mom-mom's reminded me, though, of why I had started on that path to begin with. The government had reduced her food allowance after my pop-pop passed, so she could barely afford enough food for herself each month now, let alone have extra to spare. Sharing a simple meal with me meant she was taking from her own reserves. As much as I knew she would give me the shirt off her own back if I needed it, I maintained a level of awareness to limit what I consumed. I didn't have any means to contribute at the time, and my parents were still paying for my expenses in addition to whatever extra mom-mom needed, so if we got hungry for an extra snack, it was still coming from loose change around the house. I needed to get through school and start making money.

I made it through the first year with the lowest passing GPA. Most of the great jobs were already taken on account that the windows to apply were opened to students in the order of grade point average. The only remaining job to demonstrate high potential for experience and résumé worthiness paid in prestige, meaning the ability to work there, in their eyes, was worth more than a paycheck. On a path motivated by income, my first position was unpaid. My parents provided for my monthly train pass to and from work, as well as my food allowance, and I was very thankful to have everything I needed. The office was cooler than I could have ever imagined: a high-rise office building in the middle of downtown, with ping-pong tables and lounge areas for "thought-provoking brainstorms." Much more fun than I had pictured an office environment to be. I worked harder, longer hours than some full-time employees there. My boss couldn't believe how much I could accomplish in a day. She would reward me in candy bars, like my mom-mom did for doing work around her house. Drexel was about hard work and responsibility, not partying or social events. I think that's why I felt like I fit in so well with their model. I threw myself into work so that I could learn and experience as much as I possibly could in the short six months of time I had to do it. I had no time for friends or socializing; they were too much of a distraction from my plan. My dedication and sacrifice were paying off: at the end of my six-month stay, the company offered to keep me on as a paid part-time employee. That was a high honor, so I was told, if a company asked you to stay on after a cooperative experience. I sure didn't waste the opportunity. I accepted and immediately searched for more problems to solve. My boss said I had a knack for asking questions to understand problems, and that was why the solutions I came up with worked so well. In school, they called that "collecting voice of customer." I called it listening to understand, and I didn't need a degree to teach me that. Nevertheless, it was solid validation.

I earned ten dollars an hour and felt like I was the richest person in the world. I could finally buy my mom-mom some things she needed without her having to worry about breaking into her monthly allowance. I was starting to prove that I wasn't going to be defined by my limitations, whether it be grades or my gender. I was willing to work harder and longer than anyone. That will, the willingness to give work everything I had, was what set me apart from the pack. I was offered to stay with the same company for my second cooperative rotation, but I declined so that I could broaden my experience in a different industry. Before I left, my boss said she felt it was only right to give me the truth about the place. I had this innocent impression that all of these people shared the same drive as me, that the ones who worked long hours shared a particularly common goal to succeed. The truth was that the ones who worked late together were sleeping with each other, despite the unsightly fact that they were all married and had even attended each other's weddings. The office was plagued with affairs, late-night drinking, gossip, and envy. I had kept myself at such a distance from it all I hadn't even noticed. I left feeling extremely discouraged and demotivated, wishing she had left me in blissful ignorance and wondering if anyone anywhere had any kind of pure intent to just work hard and honestly.

I was quickly coming to find that my desire for hard and honest work might have been a small-minded delusion, at least in the corporate world. My second cooperative experience was at an office in the suburbs not too far from home. I could tell my new boss liked to party, though if you judged her based on appearance, you would have thought she was more stiff than that. I saw through the facade of perfection, though, probably because I was aiming to pull off the same personal deception. She was the one who would attempt to teach me that work didn't have to be all serious. I wasn't interested in buying what she was trying to sell. About twice a week at lunchtime, a man would come visit her in her office. They would emerge together about forty-five minutes later, looking more disheveled than when they both went in. While I had a prudish mind, I wasn't senseless. I didn't know whether to feel sad for her or pity her for sleeping with a married man, unless the ring on his finger was for fashion. And in her office, of all places. She tried to get to know me despite my lack of interest. I finally accepted after she sent me a text message asking if I'd like to grab a drink to celebrate my twenty-first birthday. I didn't even know text messaging existed until then. We went out for sushi and wine; seemed like firsts for everything. I wasn't used to drinking or eating raw fish, yet I was shocked when I had to run to the bathroom to throw up in the middle of dinner. I didn't want to show signs of weakness, so I pretended nothing had happened. She was about ten years older than I was and had just about everything I wanted—a nice car, an expensive home, a good job. I guess you could say I looked up to the idea of her, which made it easier to compromise my values in order to continue hanging out with her. I had given in to the conclusion that having friends required drinking alcohol, as there wasn't one social event I was invited to without the involvement of drinking. It was a major crossroads for me. Either I would continue rejecting people from my life, or I would embrace the inevitable. I chose the latter.

We spent every weekend together after that, eating and drinking in upscale restaurants. I found myself morphing into her, wearing jeans and high heels with my collar popped like a well-dressed city girl. The look I was going after became the name my family and people in my hometown would mock me as, "city girl." For them, I was changing fast into someone they didn't know. For me, I was becoming the person I wanted to be, regardless of their approval. I started staying out all night and sleeping at her house. It was very weird at first, since she used to be my boss and asked me to sleep in her bed when I stayed. Apparently, all of her friends did that—what did I know about girl friends, since I'd never had a close one other than my sister? My mother, in particular, was enraged about it, asking me if I was gay and if she was really my girlfriend. I didn't even know what gay meant, not enough to provide a mature answer. Instead, we just fought, as all I felt from my family was another attempt to hold me back. There was no sense of encouragement from my family about what I was doing. In their eyes, every decision I made was out of pure rebellion. They didn't believe I could have the career I set out for, they didn't believe I could make the kind of money I talked about making, and they didn't believe there was a point to even trying. I lived in a town where people didn't leave. They graduated high school there, got married there, had children there, and lived out their lives on the same path as everyone before them. That just wasn't for me.

About a year into our friendship, I met a friend of hers named Brooks. He was handsome, athletic, and military mannered. I had a feeling she liked him and highly disliked the fact that he showed more interest in me than her. We exchanged numbers yet ended up mostly communicating via email every day so that we could talk during work hours. We talked about anything and everything. I couldn't wait to see his name pop up in my inbox. He was kind, respectful, always asked how my day was, and showed genuine interest in my personal goals. I wanted to know everything about him—where he grew up, what he did for a living, what his future goals were. We dated for about two years, growing distant from the group of friends that had introduced us. We had a blast together, exploring the city and making adventures. I would meet him at his place before we would go out. He lived in a high-rise apartment building that overlooked the water and had a bellman. I felt fancy going up to meet him. I was smitten watching him get ready, shaving with no shirt on and muscles so perfect they almost looked fake. I couldn't believe I could adore someone so much. His mother was coming into town for a visit, so he thought it would be the perfect time to introduce me. I knew where this was headed, since we had been talking about the idea of marriage. It was bound to come up, since the world has this standard of three dates or something before sex. I'm not sure how that dating rule came to be; however, I held strong to my belief that sex was reserved for after marriage. That was one line I was not willing to compromise. He respected that, and I cherished him for being such a gentleman. Anyhow, I knew that's where this was heading. I was so nervous about the night I hadn't eaten anything all day.

I arrived to meet his mother and her beautiful southern charm at the door. Brooks was in the kitchen preparing gin martinis and smoked salmon hors d'oeuvres. It could have been the combination of liquor and fish, or the fact that I indulged on an empty stomach, or both;

nevertheless, I had less than an hour's introduction in before becoming violently ill. Brooks was disappointed in my failure to be the woman he wanted me to be. I was embarrassed and ashamed for trying to be someone I wasn't, in the arms of someone I at least considered a friend and at most a potential life partner. In his anger, Brooks removed me from the bathroom and laid me out on his balcony, stating that his mother had to use the bathroom, so I couldn't lay in there all night. I had never felt so low or worthless. I was still sick the following morning when I tried to sneak out for a cab to take me home. Brooks insisted on driving me, to take the opportunity to make one last point on how disgruntled he was over how the night had turned out. He drove erratically, which made my already sour stomach worse, then escorted me out of his car by saying that was goodbye.

I spent two days in silence in my apartment after that—too sick to move, too angry to think about anything other than how I got there. I never wanted to drink, and I did. I never wanted to be in a relationship, and I was. Both had hurt me just like I knew they would, leaving me alone to depend on myself to pick up the pieces. I had only myself to blame. He didn't know me—well, he knew part but not enough to really know me. He knew what he saw and what I told him. He knew nothing about my family, which was still everything to me. He had met my sister and brother-in-law, but that was the extent I was willing to expose him to. He didn't know that I treasured my family's acceptance of me while I dated him, and that was one of the reasons I did date him. He didn't know that I hated the long hair he loved. He didn't know that I actually didn't like wearing heels or tight shirts. He didn't know that I didn't enjoy drinking or that I had a haunting past with it. He also didn't know that while I truly believed sex should be reserved for marriage, I had zero interest in ever having sex with him. He fell in love with a fabricated idea of me that I didn't even like. After a week or so, I found myself missing our conversations yet glad it was over. We wanted different things. I wanted him to be my best friend without any ties to intimacy, and he wanted a wife and a lover and children. I pretended for a short time, but ultimately, I just could not be that for him. As for the mutual friend we met through, she stopped talking to me as well. I received an email from her after some time of ignored messages and phone calls. She provided a nice history of my behavior over the previous year, how my drinking had become obnoxious and that it would be best to end the friendship. It stung deep. She wasn't wrong. Part of me said forget her; her behavior wasn't exactly something to model. However, the other part of me applauded her for saying no, for her courageous ability to set a healthy boundary in her life. I didn't know how to do that.

I went back to wearing baseball caps, sneakers, and athletic wear. I also shifted my full attention back on school, raised my GPA, and achieved a position during my last cooperative experience with the most sought-out company in the medical business field. They would be the third of all three companies I interned with to invite me to stay on part-time after the six-month period. Since I worked over thirty-five hours per week with each company while going to school, I was positioned to graduate with three years of professional experience, doubling the one-and-a-half-year curriculum requirement. I earned three times the amount per hour with this third position than I had with my first, providing further proof in the hope that I had the ability to make it.

After finals were finished, I celebrated with multiple consecutive games of one-on-one basketball with my brother. I came down from a layup during one of the games and landed on the side of my ankle. It blew up like a balloon so fast I could barely get my sneaker off. Instantly, I thought it was broken. I tried standing up but could not bear any weight on it. After another fight with my parents about which hospital I wanted to go to versus where they wanted to go, results of a break were inconclusive due to the swelling. I had to have it stabilized for a week until clearer scans could be taken. Eventually, it was determined that I had torn all of the major ligaments around my ankle. By the second week, my leg was covered in red, purple, and greenish bruising up to my knee, as if something much more traumatic than landing wrong on my foot had occurred. Physical therapy was mandated for three months until I could regain normal motion of my toes and strengthen my ankle to walk again. I was devastated for a number of reasons, most of all the fact that it was my right foot, my driving foot. I was stuck at home, with no way to escape, whether by foot or car.

The other overwhelming factor was that I couldn't work. I had to turn down the job offer I had initially accepted postgraduation since I was not able to drive. Everything happens for a reason, some say. The job I had originally accepted was for a business analyst, which was purely for a paycheck, as the prospect had zero excitement factor. In a way, it felt like a gift. I had the summer off for the first time in five years, which happened to also be the first time in five years I stayed still long enough to think. As I searched for other jobs, I started thinking back to a time in my life when I felt the most purpose. Caring for people who were sick and could not help themselves was where I had always felt my life had the most value. This line of thinking led to a scarier conclusion than I expected: I didn't want a career tied to the degree I had just earned. I wanted to do something that physically helped people. I wanted to serve. A sinking feeling of being stuck with a degree in business and three years of professional experience in business hit me hard. I talked to my mom about going for another degree, something in the medical field, perhaps in nursing. She was supportive while at the same time tried easing me into awareness of the $75,000 in debt I had also earned with my degree. She asked me to try to do something to start paying that off first, instead of adding to it.

I was finding great peace in the stillness, in letting go of my own expectations in exchange for trust in God to provide. I took a break from applying to jobs and spent a few weeks lounging in the sun, basking in the expectation of a more fulfilling opportunity.

With peace and gratitude,
Chole

Profits ...

Dear Addie, may this note find you well.

There was a regular crowd that hung out back of our house on what seemed like an all too frequent basis. The group consisted of my family, the neighbors in the house connected to us, and the neighbors three and four houses up the block. Up to then, I'd had school and work as a steady excuse to decline their invitations to drink and laugh at indecent jokes around a fire. Nobody gave my brother a hard time for not going out there; his decisions were never questioned and always respected. Yet my choice to distance myself was mocked, deeming me lame and snobby. During one of my quiet afternoons sunning on our deck, the next-door neighbor walked up uninvited to ask if I thought I was too good to associate with them. I told her I was and asked her in a kind, sarcastic tone to leave me alone. This was the same woman who had kissed me the night of my surprise graduation party. I neglected to tell you that story in my last letter.

College graduation was a few weeks after my injury. I had to walk the ceremony I had waited five years for in a stabilizing ankle brace and crutches. The irony was comical, as it felt like the journey itself had slightly crippled me. It turned out to be a lovely afternoon that continued with an early family dinner at an Italian restaurant in the city. When we arrived home, our deck was filled with neighbors who had already started partying on my behalf. It was the very last thing I wanted to do, yet given the party was in my honor, I obviously couldn't hide in my bedroom. I made an attempt to fit in by having a few drinks and participating in the salacious banter. I was at the table talking when the girl next door, Jules, blatantly interrupted the conversation by sitting herself on my lap. She grabbed my face and asked me if I had ever kissed a girl. When I answered no, she stuck her tongue in my mouth and proceeded to demonstrate what it was like. She was married, mind you, and my whole family watched in horror. My dad burst into the kitchen, grabbed a bottle of Grey Goose, and proceeded to chug it. He put it down and said if that was my decision, then that was that. Before I had a chance to explain I didn't ask for that, she ran into the kitchen laughing hysterically, telling us to get a grip. If my parents hadn't already thought I was a lesbian for not wanting to date, this surely cleared up any confusion.

That label irritated me so much. I could not for the life of me understand why choosing to be single was like choosing to be a leper, or apparently a lesbian. The following weeks were awkward in the neighborhood, to say the least. Jules wasn't making it any better. I tried my best to avoid running into her outside; however, that was easier said than done since our houses were literally connected. She would somehow be outside the same exact time I was, and walk inside of her house the same exact time I did. She wouldn't say much aside from a few coy words, followed by flirtatious smiles. Then, out of nowhere one day, she called me, asking questions in what felt like a random attempt to get to know me. I talked a lot about Jesus and told her most of my interests were about God. Surprisingly, she never mocked me for it. She just listened and encouraged me to do with my life what I wanted and not what other people wanted. We remained friendly, and eventually, the awkwardness from the kiss wore off.

That summer gave me a lot to think about. I felt guilty for wanting to get away from that town in such a bad way. I didn't think the people were bad; I just didn't want to end up like them. My town had a reputation for negative, pessimistic thinking. I believe it was Theodore Roosevelt who said, "Complaining about a problem without proposing a solution is called whining." That would have actually been fitting as the county slogan. Drinking and drama were the stand-ins for purposeful action. I found grumbling to be a toxin to the mind and heart, a cancer that restricted the mind to solutions one could see versus infinite trust in the impossible God could do. I guess that's what drove me to become so passionate about problem-solving. I thrived most in chaotic and problematic situations because I enjoyed doing what nobody else was doing, which was getting to the root of the issue. I never understood the point of complaining, and I certainly could not become content with such mental limits. I wanted to conquer all of the negativity, with my first target being the degrading and demoralizing things people had been saying about me and my potential. There was a rising sense of urgency to do it, too, because the constant undermining was causing a loss of trust in myself to make decisions.

I was in an ominous space between wanting to help people while simultaneously desiring to defeat their treacherous ways. After spending so much time at doctors' appointments with my family, the medical field seemed like a noble way to earn a living. I knew I wasn't smart enough to pass all of the schooling required to become a doctor, but I knew I could succeed in business. I started browsing medical business jobs and came across one posting that sounded absolutely perfect. The more I read through the description, the more in love I fell with the idea of it. When I got to the list of requirements, there was a note in bold italics that read: "We are not accepting applications from recent college graduates at this time." I had done my research—this company was preeminent in the industry. According to online reviews, if you got hired there, you would be successful anywhere in the trade. The key was getting hired, and only 10 percent of applicants passed the first stage of the interview process, and even fewer made it to hire. That was all it took, more reasons for why I couldn't do it or wasn't worthy. I had to land that job. I started talking to God again, practically begging for his help to get it. I told him I wasn't afraid of hard work and would do whatever it took. I told him I needed a sign and that if I received an offer, then I would know it was from him.

I passed the first and second interview stages pretty easily. The recruiter informed me thereafter that I was invited to a third-stage on-site interview and that more details would follow in the mail. Two days later, I received a train ticket and an agenda, solidifying that this opportunity two and a half hours away in the northern suburbs of Manhattan was actually real. I particularly enjoyed the look on people's faces when I told them that I'd be working outside of Manhattan; it carried a grandeur tone that in itself silenced people's preconceptions of my abilities. Here I was, the girl who shouldn't have even tried for a college degree, let alone think she could one day be a successful businesswoman, stepping off the train to meet a chauffeur who would drive me to the place where this journey would start. It was difficult to tell the difference between nervousness and excitement. I had never been driven in a town car before, nor treated with such respect for what I had to offer.

One of the first questions they asked when I arrived was if I was comfortable with cadavers, and I replied with a thoughtless yes without knowing what a cadaver was. I was afraid to say no to any of their questions in fear I would not get the job. I asked questions about their products and strategies that visibly challenged them, accomplishing my intent to make a strong impression. I didn't ask what the travel requirement meant or what my life would look like in a very different world away from home. I positioned myself with a fearless will to learn and a blazing drive to succeed. When I departed with an invitation to the final interview stage, I accepted with a firm handshake, confident eye contact, and a contagious smile—a sufficient sequence of nonverbal communication, I thought, to show them I was interested while hiding the fireworks of overeagerness exploding inside.

Life changed rapidly after that. I was offered the job, along with a relocation package and a salary equal to what most of the adults in my life were already making. I had absolutely no clue what I was doing, and since everyone thought I was ridiculous for considering a job so far away, I was on my own to navigate the uncharted waters. My mother and father were reluctantly by my side throughout the process, telling me all the ways this was not a good idea. Nevertheless, they did offer to cosign for a home and a car if I needed the help. It was hard to accept help in that form, help from anyone who didn't believe in me or support the help they were giving me. Help in such a form always made me feel like an obligation, like I had to prove to people that they should want to help me. Help in those terms is convenient for the giver and destructive for the receiver. If you offer help, in my eyes, there should be no expectation of repayment and no dictation of how the help should be given. It should be given selflessly as it is needed, not as a trap of guilt to hang over someone's head. Whether it was intentional or not, that's how my father always made me feel because anytime he offered help, he would make a disclaimer that his contribution was the reason I would be able to *fill in the blank*. I didn't want help from anyone who wanted credit for it. For that reason, I was deliberate in my desire for independence and reluctant to receive any kind of aid. I had nothing left for cynics and their attempts to hinder my path. I don't think they would have believed how much I craved wisdom. That's never what I was offered though. I got "it's too far," "you'll be alone," and "you can't do it on your own." Those weren't good enough reasons to reconsider; they weren't reasons at all. They were manipulative words of guilt that stirred self-doubt through my veins like poison.

The first thing I packed was the notecard. Before graduating, one of my last professors said that those who wrote down clear goals were three times more likely to accomplish them than those who didn't. I immediately wrote mine down. They were: 1. drive a nice car; 2. purchase a house before the age of twenty-five; 3. earn $85k before the age of thirty; 4. be well poised and respected. I envisioned being an international businesswoman, being the cool aunt to my future nieces and nephews, spoiling them with toys and gifts from around the world. I didn't want to be poor, fighting or worrying about money all of the time, and I didn't want to be dependent on anyone. What I wanted was to conquer oppression, sexism, and cynicism, all while loving better in the process. However, my ambition to do it all without help was not realistic. I had some credit history but certainly not enough to purchase a house. I had no choice but to accept my parents' help. This meant war. Since they were helping, they felt all of the decisions were theirs to make. If there had been even the slightest joy or excitement left in this journey, it was now gone. There would be no encouraging or guiding conversations around these decisions, only arguments about how any decision I thought to make was wrong.

I wanted a Volvo as my first car. I had done my research, and since I would be driving far distances, I wanted a car with the highest safety ratings. The prestigious brand didn't hurt either. My parents bought used cars; they said it was cheaper for the same purpose. I didn't agree. I had witnessed them waste so much money on used cars from all the random repair work needed. Naturally, they refused to sign for the new car I wanted because they thought I would be better off with a used car. There was no compromise or hearing my reasoning. They could have helped me look for a different brand, something more reasonably priced that equally satisfied my safety concerns. That didn't happen. Since their heels were in the ground, so were mine. My argument was that I could not budget for unexpected repair bills. At least with a new car, I had reassurance of reliable transportation and a predictable payment. My thought process was laughed at by all who heard it. After a few fights, my mother cosigned for my car. It was becoming evident that asking for help was a clear sign of weakness, a degrading feeling I could have gone without experiencing ever again.

As I worked with the recruiter to look for houses, I noticed another door opening. I was getting away. I was going to be able to be someone who people just met for the first time, with no preconceived notions or judgments about me. The thought of that was both freeing and terrifying. I settled on a place about halfway between my new job and home, which meant work was an hour commute and home was a one-and-a-half-hour distance. I didn't move closer to work because of my family and how they would have to drive so far when they came to visit. In our town, a twenty-minute drive was considered too far. I was leaving and still making decisions around them. They would end up visiting a mere handful of times over the course of the fourteen-year span I owned it. The commute that first month was physically and emotionally brutal. I couldn't settle on my new place until the following month after my start date, which meant a two-and-a-half-hour drive in the morning and three-hour drive home with traffic. The fact that the bonfire parties with loud music continued out back enraged me enough to actually delight in the 4:00 a.m. effort. Driven by adrenaline to get away, I worked nonstop when I got there too. Within the first week, I could tell the environment was cutthroat competitive. Opening dialogue with my new boss included a cautionary warning to exceed his expectations or become acquainted with failure. He followed with a reminder of how he had taken a chance in hiring me against the company's stance on new college graduates. Then he demoted my title and said I had to earn the one I applied for. Despite the sleep deprivation and commute disadvantage, I had to seize the opportunity to prove I was worthy of the risk he'd taken for me.

The basis of the job was product development, orthopedic reconstructive implants to be specific. It required a strong ability to speak knowledgeably with surgeons about anatomy and associated disease states. In addition, it required a technical knowledge of the tools and implants required to conduct surgery. My boss permitted me to attend a surgeon meeting during my second week, highly recommending I not speak unless spoken to. Of course, the surgeon asked me a question, and I fumbled it. My boss pulled me aside afterward and told me I could not interact with a surgeon again until I achieved the right. I was embarrassed and felt like an immediate failure. He directed me to read one hundred clinical studies on the topic of bone reconstruction and write a synopsis of each demonstrating my understanding of it. He wasn't so hard-pressed on the technical side, but I knew it was an equally weighted weakness I had to exercise. I spent the next four weeks doing two things: reading and sawing. I arrived at 7:00 a.m., allocating the first half my day to reading clinical articles and writing synopses. I spent the rest of the day until 7:00 p.m. in the bio skills room, conducting surgery on wooden practice bones, determined to know the techniques and tools better than my boss. I used my colleagues' disbelief in me as gasoline to squash their doubt and dominate. I taught myself the techniques for not only the current products but the legacy ones too. I also expanded my studies outside of the routine procedures and disease states to understand what was needed in the event something unexpected occurred during surgery. Plans are rarely executed without disruption—what made surgery any different? I hunted for the worst-case scenarios, the situations that wouldn't present during preoperative assessment and would only be found once the patient was opened. My differentiating value would be in the areas where nobody else was looking. Not only would I prevail over my colleagues' knowledge, I was going to be ten steps ahead of clinicians as well.

The day came where I was given another opportunity to attend a surgeon meeting. To my advantage, the surgeon presented a messy scenario. My colleagues might have known the primary procedure well, but they were useless if things didn't go as planned. As my peers stood incompetent, attention turned to my boss. He started thinking out loud and speaking theoretically, which visibly frustrated the surgeon. Despite being told yet again not to speak unless spoken to, I spoke up. I asked a question to clarify the situation the surgeon had found himself in, then reiterated the scenario in terms of the anatomical landscape he needed to navigate. I proceeded to unpack the problem and demonstrate how associated products could be used as an easy solution in the event of a situation like that. The surgeon expressed gratitude for the out-of-the-box thinking and for enlightening him to the other products we offered that could help in otherwise imperfect scenarios—which happened to be most of his cases. Begrudging eyes fell away when the surgeon reached out to shake my hand, saying, "That's the kind of partnership I need in the OR." Bent on survival, I found unexpected power in my approach. My peers did not have the endurance or the will to work as hard or with as much focus as I did. They spoke more than they listened and failed to follow through with helpful action. Knowing these weaknesses, I had all I needed to destroy them by dismantling their credibility.

Word spread fast that I was the go-to person to get something done. Cross-functional leaders started breaking chain of command by coming directly to me for help with solving process problems. The sales force started contending for my schedule as well, bringing me to travel between two and three cities across the country a week. Sometimes I was between multiple states in a day, supporting the more challenging cases. I was a partner in the operating room to surgeons and staff, where my opinion was sought before cutting skin or making resections. I couldn't describe the deep sense of value and worth that gave me. People who went to years of medical school were asking me to review x-rays with them, wondering if I agreed with the cuts they were about to make, or what I thought about their approach to implant placement. I was proud of myself for all of the time I had invested in learning—the hours I spent in cadaver labs dissecting every layer of muscle and tissue, navigating nerves and arteries, studying how it all worked together with boney anatomy. I was determined to know exactly how the body was designed so that I knew how to reconcile it all after disease had threatened to destroy natural intent. I checked off two of my notecard goals, moving from a liability to an asset in less than six months. Superseding my expectations was that people of influence and power valued me. It was more than I could have dreamed or planned.

With peace and gratitude,
Chole

... And Losses

Dear Addie, may this note find you well.

The value and worth I was feeling were not translating to the contentment and peace I ultimately desired. Esteem was more fleeting than I had imagined it would be, not to mention far less practical toward supplying basic needs. As exhausting as traveling was, it helped alleviate the stress on my food budget. Between a mortgage payment, car expenses, and student loans, I had just enough left for a diet of frozen vegetables. It was tough to swallow, the fact that I was working so hard and not able to afford more substantial provisions for myself. Expensing meals was a perk I started to depend on. I posted pictures on social media of all the places I went and the various foods I tried, to promote an adventurous and wealthy perception of my new life. It helped hide the fact that I was otherwise broke and hungry. For those closer in physical proximity to my life, the perk of having a chauffeur pick me up and drop me off for all trips aided as an affirmative veil over my deficiencies. Diverting attention away from the truth was easy; however, it didn't change the facts of reality. I could not shake a sense of emptiness that each of my plans failed to fill. My neighbors were all very kind and invited me to gather with them often, but my schedule was so unpredictable I couldn't commit to dinner a week in advance if I tried. I didn't mind the chaotic schedule excuse because I also wanted to keep my distance. I knew I could only talk about work so much before personal questions would organically follow, and I couldn't allow that. I had to control what people knew about me and how they perceived me. One person outside of my family knew something about my home life, Emma, who only knew because she had witnessed the discord when visiting on the weekends. I met her through Lucy and stayed in touch with both of them after senior week. Emma didn't judge and mostly offered empathy. She was the closest thing I had to an ally. I didn't trust anyone else to get too close.

It didn't dawn on me back then that I wasn't making an effort to settle in my new hometown. I just kept running back to what I knew. I worked and traveled all week, then rushed south to my parents' almost every Friday night for the weekend. Despite our challenges, I missed my family a lot after I moved. More than that, though, I missed an idea of family relationship that never paired with actuality. I'd drive down each weekend with the expectation that everyone would be sitting around sharing food and laughing, having good, innocent fun. And if I'm honest, that's usually how it started. Everyone enjoyed one another's company until excessive drinking turned loving relations into hateful discord, predictably engrossing any and all joy that was had. I continued to make the trip down each weekend; however, instead of spending time with my family, I would hang out with Emma, doing what I didn't want to do, which was go to bars. My brother had largely taken my place in caring for my mom-mom, which I felt guilty for. I still helped on the weekends, but it was nowhere near the union we'd had before I moved away. Monday morning always came quickly. The long drive back north meant I had three hours to process each weekend before the week started. I couldn't articulate the *why* behind it, I could just feel a disconcerting internal tear. My mom-mom was my best friend, and I was trading her companionship for selfish mischief. Adding to the guilt of living so far away was the realization that I was also hiding from my family. I was a totally different person up north, which my family knew nothing about. There was a certain point on the highway, about twenty miles out, where I would start to feel a noticeable weight lift from my shoulders. It was about that same point coming south that I would morph back into that anxious and angry little girl they all knew so well, so in the grand scheme of things, nothing ever changed.

It was around March when travel picked up even more—another multicity trip in a week's span of time that ended with a few cases in Flint, Michigan. I landed in Newark on a Friday night to a string of text messages from some colleagues asking me to come out for a drink. As I slowly walked through the terminal to meet my driver, I contemplated what extending the night would mean. I replied, stating how tired I was, only to receive pressuring rebuttal to compromise my state of mind and socialize. All I wanted to do was go home and go to bed, and while that was exactly what I needed, I fed into the peer pressure. I was so concerned with being labeled antisocial and unapproachable that I went in order to prove that's not who I was. By the time I arrived, all that was left of the crowd were a few stragglers from happy hour. They handed me a glass of wine and talked about how much they disliked their jobs. I distinctly remember looking around, wondering what I was doing there. Nobody cared that I had made the effort after the week I'd had; I was just another person to drown their sorrows with. It wasn't worth it; after a glass of wine and half a beer, I decided to leave. On my way out, I heard remarks like I was too good for them, which by that point had no effect on me. They were just pitiful ploys to get me to stay well beyond my limits without a single care for my well-being. I hadn't eaten dinner and was approaching debilitating fatigue; all I could focus on was getting home as fast as I could. I was a forty-five-minute drive away at that point, mostly highway, which meant at eighty miles per hour, I could be there in no time. It was after 11:00 p.m. when I started the drive home, and having previously driven in similar states of sleepy inebriation, I didn't think twice about this attempt. About ten minutes into the drive, I was on the open highway with my bed in sight. My eyes fell so heavy that I could barely make out which lane I was in. I remember glancing at my dashboard and seeing I was at seventy-five miles per hour when suddenly I hit something. To this day, I do not know what I hit. I just remember being too carelessly tired to stop. Not too long after that, the dark night sky lit up with red and blue flashing lights.

I was pulled over and pulled out of my vehicle. The officer asked me a series of questions, to which I complied and answered each one. I told him how tired I was and that all I wanted to do was go home. I was dressed in a suit, a suit coat, and heels, unchanged from my work trip. He asked me to walk a straight line, and I remember knowing I couldn't do it. As I fell short of success with each step, I blamed my heels and previously injured ankle for my inability to balance. After my third failed attempt, the officer yanked me fiercely from the roadside and shoved me against my car. He stripped off my coat and tossed it onto the highway. That dress coat was my favorite, a gift from my parents when I got the job. I remained totally silent and compliant as he pulled my arms behind my back, tightening the handcuffs so much that I could feel the steel cutting into my skin. I timidly asked if he could loosen them, and he screamed in reply, shouting obscenities and taunting me about how I was some rich girl who thought I could get away with my recklessness. Little did he know I could barely afford the drinks that had landed me in the situation. Just over six months into the life I had dreamed of, I found myself in the back of a police car, facing an abrupt end to it all.

When we arrived at the police station, I was put into a cell with a small metal bed and cover that felt more like a steel wool scouring pad than a blanket—a far cry from my eight-hundred-dollar, king-size comforter set at home. I could barely afford food yet had no problem accumulating credit card debt for material items, like that comforter set, which lent to the illusion of wealth. The officer approached the holding cell to administer a breathalyzer. After two negative blows, he asked me to take a deeper breath and blow from my belly. Tired and unaware of my rights, I complied until he gained a positive result. Once he got what he wanted, he handed me my phone through the bars and permitted one call. Extremely embarrassed for anyone to know, I reluctantly called home. My father answered—he was drunk, with music blasting in the background. When I told him what had happened, he laughed and said how foolish I was to have gotten caught. He handed the phone to my mother. I told her where I was and what had happened, and she said she was too afraid to drive so far in the dark, especially without my dad. His selfishness never failed to disappoint, yet this was a whole new level. I had never felt so forsaken. The pain of hostile love struck my heart like a scalpel in a cognizant state. I was convinced then and there that every statement of "I love you" was, at its core, a rotten set of selfish and meaningless words.

The officer granted me another call as I sobbed. I decided to call Emma, who at 1:00 a.m. actually answered, and moreover spent the next three hours driving to come bail me out. It was not convenient for her, nor was it easy, yet she did it. While I waited for Emma's rescue, I lay in the fetal position on the metal bed under the steel wool blanket, contemplating how someone I barely knew was more willing to come help me than my own family. She took me to a diner after she picked me up—it had to have been almost five o'clock in the morning at that point. I ordered chicken fingers so that she wouldn't have to eat alone, yet I couldn't bear to take more than a bite. I hardly spoke a word either, never so void of thought and emotion in my life. When we got back to my place, I made her a bed on the couch, then went back to my room, locked the door, and stood in the shower, hoping the hot water would wash away the film of disgrace on my skin. No amount of scrubbing could make me feel clean. I took a dose of NyQuil and went to bed. I woke up just a few hours later with an extraordinary sense of relief that it had all been a nightmare. It only took about a minute for me to sit up and realize the cruel blunder. I walked out to greet Emma, who appeared to have hardly slept herself. She asked me how I felt. I mumbled an "Okay, I guess," when what I really felt was a sense of guilt coursing through my veins like poison. I silently recalled the countless times I had driven drunk up to that point, and it was making me physically sick.

She offered to drive me to my parents', who ironically asked us to meet them at a local bar, where they were having an early dinner with their friends. The last thing I wanted to be around was alcohol, and I was still hurt by their response to my call the night before. I didn't want to go at all, but at the same time, I didn't know where else to turn. When we got there, my parents' friends offered me a drink and told me to relax, then started telling stories from their past with drinking and driving that were apparently humorous. The attempt to normalize the reckless behavior seriously astonished me. I started talking about how bad it was, how much damage there was to my car, and how I could have killed someone or myself. My father's laughter and repeated words of "it's your fault you got caught" further provoked my devastated heart. His arrogance toward the situation brought me back to the countless nights he had driven us drunk when we were kids. I hated him for having been so reckless with our lives, and now here I was, no better. I went out that night with full awareness of my exhaustion, then willingly ingested alcohol on an empty stomach, all for the sole purpose of avoiding social rejection. I furthermore got behind the wheel because I was convinced that I was fine to drive. I couldn't possibly relinquish control of how and when I went home. At the center of each decision I made that night was me. Nothing about that is normal. I didn't even consider the impact of my actions on another human life, let alone my own, which made me wonder how I myself could even remotely love another person. I surely didn't love God enough to revere with precious precaution the life he had created. While everyone around me seemed content deemphasizing what I had done, I started to question why God had allowed me to survive it.

Monday came, and I was in a state of panic. I had to call out sick in order to give myself more time to come up with a reason as to why I would soon no longer be able to drive in the state I worked and lived in. My mother had driven me back north that morning to collect my impounded car. It was hard to conceive that I had continued driving after the impact, given the amount of damage. My mother stood next to me in front of the wreckage and muttered, "You should thank God you survived." She wasn't angry with me, nor did she demean me in any way. She just stood next to me and accompanied me through the process. Since I could remember, I had fought to save her from the destruction caused by alcohol. I didn't deserve her merciful support now, being yet another person she loved to hurt her with alcohol abuse. As much as I despised myself for having her there to see firsthand what I had done, I needed her. I needed my mother to hold me and tell me that everything was going to somehow be all right. And that's exactly what she did. Then she dropped me off so that she could make the far drive before the sun went down.

I couldn't afford more disappointment in my life, nor could I allow this one lapse of judgment to ruin everything I had worked and fought for. Probably even more so, I could not give those who doubted me the pleasure of gloating at my failed expense. In a fit of dismay, I began exploring all transportation options to get from my house to work. Forty minutes outside of Manhattan, I was shocked to find that there was no line of public transportation whatsoever between where I lived and where I worked. I called a few taxi companies next, which ended up being far more expensive than I could afford. I even called the chauffeur who drove me when I traveled, thinking he would provide some sort of discount, given the volume of business my company gave him. That, too, was equally unaffordable. As I sat on my bedroom floor, crying hysterically with my head between my knees, I noticed how swollen my ankle was. I lifted my head as if an actual light bulb appeared. I realized I could conceal my grievous mistake with a sympathetic injury and even convinced myself that it wasn't a total lie since I was still struggling with it at times. It didn't solve my transportation problem; however, ankle surgery was a more noble reason for not being able to drive than a DWI. I walked into the office on Tuesday with a slight limp, wearing my old ankle brace. When people rushed to see what had happened, I told them I aggravated an old ankle injury over the weekend that now required surgery to repair. I tried to downplay it while simultaneously adding a layer of victimized devastation for blameless effect. A guy I casually said hi to in the hallway appeared suddenly in the conversation and said, "I carpool from your area. You are more than welcome to join us until you can drive again." Desperate times call for desperate measures, as they say. I didn't enjoy lying; it was just the only way I knew how to survive, given the circumstances. I jumped on his offer, and I thanked him profusely for his kindness and mercy. My lie was so plausible I started to believe I was actually getting surgery soon. The best way I knew how to fight back in this type of scenario was by deflecting accountability and regaining control of perception by projecting myself as the injured party. I executed that act all too well.

With peace and gratitude,
Chole

Survival

Dear Addie, may this note find you well.

There was no act or facade convincing enough to mislead my parents in who I was. Once I solidified my public survival strategy, I felt a bit more at ease to privately face reality. I wouldn't say it was peace I felt, more like blind ignorance to the unknown facts ahead that held plausible potential to change the course of my life. I think my parents were more afraid for my future than I was. Not that I was prepared to face the worst-case scenario, I was just arrogantly courageous in my unwillingness to face discipline. I was also angry at my parents for their help. I didn't want them to be the ones supporting me in this because it felt like they were just there to say, "I told you so." I didn't expect to be coddled or for anyone to have empathy for me. Laying more disappointment on me didn't feel right either though. I was especially bitter toward my father for the fact that I was facing a punishment he too deserved but never received. It was one thing to get arrested and call home for help. It was a whole other thing to reach a drunk, incompetent voice on the other end mocking you for your mistake, now to have that same voice represented as some kind of honorable hero abating in your correction. All it did was further aggravate an already hostile spirit within me.

I have clouded memories of waking up on that sunny March morning, preparing coffee in a deadened state, trying to grasp the vulgar nightmare that was my life. I didn't eat breakfast; the looming unknown of what the day would release had my stomach in knots. Such a stark contrast to the sense of stability in the world provided by the clear sky and crisp air. When we arrived at the courthouse, I met the lawyer my mother and father had hired for me. He approached us, addressing my parents first to reassure them that he had everything under control. Then, utterly emotionless, he turned toward me with instructions to not speak except to plead guilty. The man hadn't known me for more than thirty seconds, and yet there I was entrusting my entire future to him. I watched his every move from a despondent tower as he stood between me and a penalty that would derail life as I knew it. The sentencing recommendation was harsher than a first-time offense, due to the high BAC and wrecked state of my vehicle at the time of my arrest. I was facing thirty to ninety days in prison, a $10,000 fine, twelve months of a suspended driver's license, and mandatory alcohol education classes. When the judge called my case forward, I turned to look at my parents and caught my mother silently crying. I had never felt shame so inseparable.

The judge asked me how I'd like to plea, to which I replied, "Guilty," just as I was advised. The lawyer gestured toward me when he began to speak, as if I was a letter and he was Vanna White. He painted the picture of a responsible young woman, new homeowner to the state, family oriented with my parents present, facing the loss of a promising career in a distinguished industry because of a transitory loss of judgment. He continued turning toward my parents, using their distraught disposition as a backdrop to his monologue. He gave an account of their earnest lifestyle, further adding of their selfless compassion exhibited by their willingness to travel so far so early in the morning to support their struggling child. In closing, he made the state's proposed penalty seem inconceivable, pleading my innocence as if any charges against my driving record were absurd. The judge turned toward me with a resigned look on his face, as if he didn't agree with what was about to come out of his own mouth. He suspended my driver's license for six months and issued five mandatory sessions of Alcoholics Anonymous. I didn't feel as grateful as one would think I should. I didn't feel much of anything at all, except deeper anger.

Where I expected to find punishment in solitary confinement, I found collateral beauty and a gentle kind of discipline. The carpool opened my eyes to the fact that some people could be dependable and trustworthy. It was actually kind of nice, being with people in a community sense. I also enjoyed the fact that I could decline social events with a solid excuse that didn't leave me feeling guilty. Outside of work, my only mode of transportation was a bicycle, which meant I couldn't go too far or carry too much. I could only forage what I could fit in a backpack. It was delightful, really. There were a few farm stands nearby that I discovered on weekends, where twenty dollars would provide a week's worth of fruits and vegetables. It was gracefully simplistic, a forced period of survival that demanded a mindful state of presence—a rarity for me back then. I had been spending every ounce of energy I had on being ahead, living in the next step. There had been no time to pause, let alone allot to God. The involuntary stillness provided a unique opportunity to admire his world and further contemplate my place in it. A verse from Psalm 23 was at the forefront of my mind, "He makes me lie down in green pastures, he leads me beside quiet waters." I didn't know scripture well and had never had a real interest in engaging it. The Bible always made me feel frustrated, overwhelmed, and inadequate. I only knew the verses I found to be inspiring and encouraging. Nevertheless, the idea of God laying out this green pasture for me was intriguing. A serene break from the rush, restricted from trouble yet free to roam the land with pure enjoyment. It was enchanting to ponder the gentle breezes as I pedaled to be the movement of God's spirit. As for the weekends I got a ride back to my parents', my state of mind was polar opposite.

The two words that best describe how I felt at home were incomplete and rejected. I wholeheartedly believe that nobody intentionally desired for me to feel that way; it's just the nature of the beast who seeks to kill and destroy love. It's not hard to feel rejected when the people you want acceptance from the most belittle every decision you make and every dream you have. Even something as simple as cutting my hair short stirred hostile relations. Apparently, I severed my identity as a woman by cutting off my long, curly hair.

It is equally easy to feel incomplete when you're told so many times that you are, as is. My parents and my grandparents told me that my "troubled" nature derived from my singleness and that all of my longings would be satisfied if I just met a man and got married. My accomplishments, like graduating from a college with a strenuous curriculum and establishing a lucrative career, were not good enough. They had expectations for my life that I could not submit to, and failing to meet those expectations meant I was an absolute disappointment. It was a lose-lose situation. The DWI was further proof for them that the path I had chosen was the wrong one, solidifying the case for me to accept a life I didn't want. Somehow, marriage and having children would not only bring me peace but also promote a state of happiness and worthiness I could not obtain otherwise. Without a life path outline similar to theirs, I was apparently lost and disturbed. They couldn't see how confused it made me to think that a man was the solution to my thirst for life, or that the cultural characteristics that define a female were the answer to my identity search. I surely didn't allow anyone to see that this inevitably made me feel like without a man, I was incapable of receiving love. Caustic pressure mounted to an uncontrollable point, with no place to release it. I had to prove I was worth love and acceptance on my own accord, without a man. Thus, man became the next opposition I had to extinguish.

As time went on, I buried myself deeper into work. I was sleeping in hotels more nights than my own bed and starting to see some aspects of corporate culture that both amazed and alarmed me. I was working closer with sales, continuing to assist in surgeries in addition to supporting business dinners. The more time I spent on the social side of the business, the more aware I became of how the industry operated— behind the scenes, that is. Being in the operating room all day made the trade seem noble. I thrived on problem-solving and the rush of assisting the surgeons in figuring out how to reconstruct unexpected anatomic disasters. I couldn't mentally link what we did in the daytime to what ensued at night. Entertainment was a new element of work for me; I didn't know what I didn't know. There was drinking and drugs, strip clubs, kickback deals, and sexual debauchery like something out of a movie—all of the things I despised, combined and completely socially acceptable. I wasn't used to that. Where I came from, drinking led to fist fights and bloody noses in backyards and places where drinks cost two dollars each. That was the glaring difference between corrupt behavior across the social classes. I was far from innocent in the train of thought, beginning to absorb the shared hypocritical perception. The drunken, defiling talk disgusted me at home around a case of Miller Lite yet took on a seductive and dominant feel when dressed in expensive attire with an exquisite backdrop.

The combination of intelligence and wealth essentially entitled the loose behavior. "Work hard, play hard" was the motto, and it was starting to make rational sense. The money, along with the arrogance, was earned, I guess. It was some kind of cross to bear, working twelve-hour shifts, with each minute demanding meticulous attention to detail, where any level of negligence could severely impact another human's life. It's no wonder some in the medical profession perceive themselves to be like gods. The industry played to that exact mental chorus, providing access to the lawlessness necessary to counter the tension. Conversation at these two-thousand-dollar dinners focused on custom-designed Porsches, vacation homes, and boasting about the ideas executed earlier in the day that dominated the minds of all. The surgeons were to be venerated above all other humans at these events, while everyone else was to do whatever it took to keep them happy. We went to five-star restaurants and exclusive clubs, from Manhattan to Las Vegas and every major city in between. I spent countless nights as the only woman smoking cigars and sipping whiskey in an effort to blend in as an equal to the men. Even the internal idea of entertainment was extravagant. Meetings organized for continuous sales education appeared to be more like after-parties to movie premieres. Entire resorts were rented out, alcoholic beverages and energy drinks were steadily in reaching distance, and the push to make more money was endlessly at the forefront of all dialogue. It was a ruthless environment where carefully calculated, aggressive personalities competed to get whatever they desired—an indigenous lesson on the influence generated by money, power, and sex.

There is no course in college, or address on Sundays, for that matter, to help one navigate such terrain. Adding to the callous culture was the fact that it was a male-dominated industry. Women typically played more of a supporting role, as eye candy. Many thought I was too naive to recognize the division between genders; however, they didn't know how I grew up. I was fully aware that men thought that their contributions in life were greater than those of women. They didn't know that my passion was motivated by my determination to beat them at their own game. When I was called out to surgeries and business dinners on the merit of my technical expertise and relational deftness, I played into that as well. I pretended to be flattered by the opportunity, then entered each operating room with a calm, collected, confident approach. Once inside, I held the power to destroy their credibility. I knew each product to its most intricate technical specification, even those several generations old. I knew exactly how to revise each and anticipate risks and challenges, completely armed with solutions that would stoke the surgeon's ego-driven execution. I knew the anatomy equivalent to the surgeon, including how the kinematics responded to a reconstructed environment. I guided them through cases in a way that addressed problems before they could even become questions. In the minds of some, I was creating an indispensable role for myself. I defied the stereotypical woman while simultaneously proving that men weren't the only ones who could enact manual dexterity and mechanical aptitude. However, what I had in grit and knowledge was not translating to what I needed in my bank account. I was executing the work that ultimately brought the male reps more recognition and remuneration.

It was a genius hustle, really. They played to my wants and needs just like I watched them do with customers. They preyed on my dedication and determination, knowing that calling a rookie like me to save the day would not only help their business but simultaneously be the ego boost I needed to feel essential. Somehow, they determined I had a need to feel important, and they weren't wrong. I was hopping on planes within hours' notice some days, dropping everything to help in tumultuous cases or present at major hospital accounts. I was so focused on beating them with a principled approach, working to gain respect and establish authentic relationships with their customers that I didn't realize I was being played too. They didn't care about their credibility; they were profiting in rich abundance. Their approach to manipulate and consume was disingenuous, hidden in plain sight. And by all accounts, their way was winning. I genuinely cared about those surgeons and their patients. I didn't treat them like they were above me or beneath me, I treated them equally, with reverence for each of our roles in the trade. Those doctors were hunted and stalked by reps all day long, vying for their business like desperate vultures. The infamous elevator pitch looked more like a piteous pursuit-and-ambush effort in real life. I couldn't imagine how annoying that would be, nor could I imagine having to basically beg for work. I had no interest in selling them anything or getting anything from them; I just wanted to help. Maybe my heart was in the right place, or maybe there was no place for integrity and fortitude in this line of work. More apparent was the latter, causing me to become more like an exploited asset than budding potential.

The harder I worked, only to watch other people's income grow, was frustrating, to say the least. Something else started to become clearer as well: my male counterparts were being promoted without coming close to achieving the knowledge and skill set I had developed. My devotion was meaningless without a penis. Our bills were more complimentary than our paychecks. And trust me, I was not looking to be promoted because of my gender. I would actually be mortified to receive any sort of recognition on the sole basis of my being a woman; that would be a complete erosion of my character and capability. Yet that was what I was up against, at home and now in the world. Regardless of my ability to circumvent the cultural ceilings of the industry, virtue and humility just weren't proving to be practical partners in success. I began considering a transition into sales so I could compete on a more direct playing field, as well as make more money. I was basically performing the job already anyway. The more I thought about it, though, I realized I didn't want to be associated with the character that a sales title presumed. As much as I craved the income, it wasn't enough of a victory in the end. I wanted more.

I began to recall how I had created my initial value by taking the road of most resistance, the road that demanded absolute devotion in order to incapacitate my competition. I started filling my time in between travels with certificate training courses, in search of knowledge that would extend beyond what I had achieved from a technical and anatomic standpoint. Having that level of expertise showed me that I could control certain circumstances with a specific proficiency, yet that was only a mere taste of what was possible if I had a greater breadth of influence. I felt as though expanding in these areas would also help me stabilize my life, which had just too easily flown off the rails. Being peer pressured and underestimated was fueling an internal fire of anger and resentment—I didn't want to be the victim I portrayed my own self to be. Emotional intelligence therefore became my new obsession, particularly because it opened a door to an arsenal of tools I could use to control many situations. I didn't want to just survive anymore; I wanted to thrive. I set a new objective in an effort to take control of my life: I would become the huntress instead of the prey.

With peace and gratitude,
Chole

Conformity

Dear Addie, may this note find you well.

In the culture I was immersed in, it was hard to be a huntress without some element of seductive tactics on my tool belt. What an interesting topic sex is, to that point. Poisonous yet enticing. Scandalous yet sacred. My modesty and your arrogance on the subject harmonized as seamlessly as oil and water. It frustrated me to my core that you formed an understanding of me on the basis of perception rather than truth, carelessly censoring questions and never grasping the danger in such blatant short-sightedness. You were so convinced you knew me better than I knew myself, further treating me like some fragile puritan who required a leisurely escort into a world you deemed yourself a champion of. I allowed it, observing in rare form how you were the only human on earth I was reluctant to destroy for miscalculating my ability. If you'd dared to ask, you would have discovered that sex was not a topic ever formally talked about in my life. That wasn't why I didn't speak about it with you, though. It has been my experience that people who talk about it a lot don't really do it much. Speaking about it was never going to change my mind on whether I would do it or not; it was either already going to happen or there was no chance. There was no middle ground, and if it had to be discussed, the only question being sought to answer was why it wasn't happening. I guess that is why you had to talk about it. If you were a man, I would have deemed the incessant discourse to be a pathetic attempt to plead adequacy in an effort to mask incompetence. I gave you the benefit of the doubt because you didn't know any better.

In a less sinister sense, talking about it was also a violation of the fading flair of inviolable mystery. This was the chasm I attempted to balance on the matter. That, and the fact that my family raised me to be very discreet. My father never approached such substance with me, my mother instilled fear at the thought of engaging in such relations outside of marriage, and forget it ever being addressed at church. Church was the one place I wish it had been discussed, though, because I would have liked to know what God thought about it. Particularly since it was culturally characteristic that the ultimate goal of every date was either sex or a step toward it, with an underlying distinction amid the aspiration where men were perceived as domineering and women as dissolute. On the flip side, if you were a virgin, you were ostracized as a stuffy prude. I was always proud of being a stuffy prude. I transformed into an escape artist whenever a relationship got close to getting too close like that. I never felt emotionally safe enough to share how I felt about sex. The thought of expressing the fact that I had zero interest in even kissing a man made me feel like an outcast of society. I didn't possess the sense of attraction that other people talked ad nauseam about; nor did I have an appetite to willingly permit another person to have such control. If anything repelled me more than the thought of getting pregnant, it was that—allowing a man to have any level of dominion over me.

Aside from my convictions against marriage and parenthood, I also believed sex was reserved for procreation between married people. That's as much as I gathered on God's intentions for it from the Old Testament reading lessons on Sundays. Regardless of what God instructed, it clearly manifested outside of the boundaries of marriage. Yet nobody wanted to talk about that part of reality, especially not at church. You would think, if it was that big a deal in the matter of life and death, it would be talked and taught about. Maybe people were too embarrassed to discuss their impure desires. Or maybe, like me, people were afraid of being judged for desiring the opposite of everyone else. Either way for me, avoiding it was always the dependable choice.

Despite an absent craving to indulge, there was a fascination brewing within me around the power sex could possess. The way multitudes of people within my profession normalized the otherwise disgraceful behavior led me to wonder if what was written in the Bible was ancient, outdated wisdom. I wondered how so many people could behave in opposition to how God might otherwise have it, and how masses of people could all have it wrong. Holding firm to my convictions about sex, I began to analyze other aspects of persuasion that could possess the same influence without actually committing the act. Figuring out a balance was an utter necessity because sex and seduction were becoming unavoidable forms of career currency.

One of the most impactful tools I gathered from emotional-intelligence training was the significance of listening to understand. That, in itself, had power. Most people listen to respond, despite our innate desire to be heard and understood. I remember sitting through countless sales trainings where it was taught to speak 20 percent of the time and listen 80 percent of the time, and how the majority of people do the exact opposite. It opened my ears to my own flaws. I listened half-heartedly, holding fervently to a superior reply until it was my turn to speak. I didn't care to understand. I just cared to prove that my opinion was right and that I knew more than my conversing opponent. I even interrupted people when their point wasn't going in the direction I wanted it to. Comprehending my relational limitations was better than finding gold. It helped me realize how virtually impossible it was to truly solve a problem by half listening to the issues, then tearing into them like a bull in a china shop. Learning how to get to the root of problems was like finding out I had a second brain I'd been neglecting to tap into. I became particularly attentive to how half-hearted listening was why so many solutions were proposed to solve mere symptoms of real issues. At work, I started to swap overbearing factual statements for meticulously articulated questions. Albeit factual, presumptive statements like that still perpetuated assumptions. Questions, on the other hand, invited intention and protection from premature presumption. Nobody wants to be told they are wrong; we need to figure it out on our own. My new training helped me maintain my goal while achieving greater success with just a small tweak in approach. Rather than forcing someone to appear irrelevant, I started asking questions that would create the space for them to be futile in their own voice.

I expanded my studies in my personal time to learn about character assessment. I wanted to know every detail, from reading a room to reading individuals before they even spoke. Having lenses to assess emotional threats and weaknesses, in addition to character and competency, was a whole new set of ammunition I couldn't wait to bolster. Achieving the ability to understand the whys behind people's preferences and the physical body language that spoke what words didn't was like learning a new language. It was a higher level of communication that served as a collection of unassailable signposts. I could use the signals to help me love someone better, or better yet, coerce them toward what I wanted to use them for—circumstantially dependent, of course.

The first opportunity to use these new tools in my personal life came sooner than I expected. I was growing so bitter and resentful toward my family I couldn't even fake a smile at gatherings anymore. My disappointment rating with them was increasing, too, as I failed to execute duties as my only sister's maid of honor. I was traveling so much that I had no time to help plan her wedding shower. If I'm honest, I wish she wouldn't have chosen me at that time in my life. I was a horrible maid of honor for her. I was a horrible sister too. Anyway, the idea of sitting around for hours, making small talk and playing trivial games with people who might have known my sister and brother-in-law on the surface at best held zero value to me. Bridal and baby showers always seemed like the most unauthentic exchange of human relation to exist. That mental position didn't help motivate me to be involved in the little downtime I had; rather it added to my desire to avoid it all together. So, you can imagine that I wasn't the most anticipated guest. All of the girls in the bridal party despised me for leaving the planning responsibilities to them, while my mother abhorred me, with nagging guilt about how discouraging my contributions were. I said a few hellos, then bought a six-pack of overpriced beer and segregated myself by the bar. I felt so out of place. I felt more comfortable in loneliness than I did in the company of familiar strangers. Just as my soul was stirring for a major insurrection, a familiar voice asked to join me.

It was Jules, the girl next door. Well, she wasn't my next-door neighbor anymore, but she was still my parents', and now my sister's, as she and my brother-in-law had bought a house on the same street. We got to talking, and after a series of questions, I deemed her to be as proportionately out of place as I was. I joked and asked her if God's idea for marriage involved grown women wrapping one another in toilet paper wedding gowns for fun. She asked me about what I did for a living and shared how she was going back to school to be a nurse in the same line of work. She told me about her rebellious teenage years and why she married so young. Clearly, a man wasn't what fulfilled her life either. We had a fun little private party playing music on the jukebox, dancing, and drinking. It was refreshing to feel relatable to someone. I could see us being friends, which was far from what I previously thought of her. She was loud, obnoxious, in your face, and the one all the men in the neighborhood talked about. It infuriated my mother, along with the other wives on the block. Useless arguments stirred by meaningless jealousy. They would talk about her body as if she was an object, what they would do to her and so on. None of them wanted to leave their wives, just perverted talk like they were pubescent boys drooling over a girl way out of their league. I found it to be pathetic. Her husband was no different. When I lived there, like a creep, he used to watch me wash my car out back, and when I was out for a run, he would show up randomly on my path and shamelessly hit on me. All of that added to the angst I had toward men and the entitlement they asserted over women.

I missed the memo that there was a multi-house after-party on the block. It was an opportune time to depart back north, but I'd had too much to drink to make the long drive home safely. I headed to the bathroom at the restaurant before leaving for my parents', angry at myself for once again giving alcohol control over my circumstances. As I turned to lock the door, I felt the doorknob rotate in the opposite direction and the door forcefully open in on me. It was Jules—she had followed me to the bathroom and locked the door behind herself. If I had any sense, I would have feared what was about to happen. It was the only women's room on the floor, and a single room at that. Walking out together already wrote the story. She threw herself on me and started intensely kissing me. I laughed most of the time and kept asking what she was doing. That didn't stop her. As I tried to comprehend what was going on, a sudden rush of scenes played in my mind like a movie. I saw all of the arrogant men in my life, particularly the ones unappreciative of their wives, lusting after other women. In that moment, I gained a startling interest in seeing where this would go. We left together, omitting any and all consequences. The secrecy had a dangerous draw of covert reprisal, until we finally got caught once in the bathroom of my sister's basement. I had never seen my sister so angry at me before. She commanded us to leave, and I can still remember the feeling of how deep that stung. I felt it even then, in my inebriated state. I knew I had to be entertaining something pretty bad for my sister to kick me out of her home.

We walked back down the street to my parents' house. I wanted to go to bed and forget the day ever happened, but I blew that option too. We walked in the front door and found my parents in the living room, noticeably disturbed by my behavior. My father repeatedly accused me of being a lesbian, while my mother simultaneously offered a rather gruesome depiction of what that identity meant—each stumbling over each other's words to warn of the unnatural choice I was engaging in. I was even more inebriated by that point, yet just sensible enough to accumulate the weight of more dejection. Feeling exceptionally grotesque in my parents' presence, I allowed her hand to grasp mine as she pulled me outside. We lay on the grass on the front yard and gazed at the stars for a while, pondering what normal was. I asked Jules what she thought God thought of it all, to which she replied there was no such thing as normal in this world. She asked me to come into her house, which I knew would cause more trouble for me with my family, given the houses were literally connected. I thought about it for a moment, then recounted the recent scene inside—I was a troubled, improper, and immoral girl with no chance of gaining approval or acceptance from the people who claimed to love me unconditionally. I had no place to sleep at that point, so I conceded with nothing left to lose.

Jules reached her hand across the grass and softly clasped it around mine to lead me in. It was mind-numbingly twisted how safe her gentle touch made me feel. Bordering the line of adulteress was where I felt emotionally safe on that street, not one door over, in the home I grew up in. Something was extraordinarily wrong with that; even as intoxicated as I was, I could understand that much. She held loosely to my hand as she closed the curtains and escorted me up the steps. I stopped at the top of the staircase and told her I couldn't go any further. I expressed how wrong it was and how her bed was meant for her and her husband. We sat there on the steps for a while longer in silence before she got up to go talk with him. She came back out to get me, leading me tenderly into their room. I remember trembling in fear as my feet entered, like I had just bit on an appealing but toxic lure. She convinced me that it wasn't cheating if her husband approved, which he did without hesitation. In that moment as I crossed the threshold of the doorway into the room, I felt a distinct shift in my spirit as chastity began to transform into a contaminated desire to devour. Overcome with hurt, animosity, and resentment, I proceeded to passionately perform every physical desire she had, in front of her husband, for five nonstop hours.

After she fell asleep, I found myself lying in a paralyzing state of bewilderment, staring out of the front windows to a familiar street scene, contemplating what I had just done. I couldn't fathom it or understand where that part of me had just come from. I hadn't taken any bodily enjoyment from it; that much was clear. I only remember having a sense of satisfaction that was deeper in my soul, completely separate from any sensual response. The sun was close to rising by that point, and I wanted nothing more than to get out of there as fast as I could without anyone seeing me. The tone in that house took a notable shift on my way out, as if what was done at night could literally not exist in the daylight. I left at dawn without any sleep for the three-hour drive back north.

I drove in silence, making two stops along the way, one for coffee and one to home for a shower and change of clothes. I had to wear a turtleneck in late spring to cover the carnal markings on my skin. I felt defiled and further from God than I ever had before. As I drove, I pondered what punishment waited for me for breaking yet another one of the Ten Commandments. By the time I arrived at the office, it felt like half the day had passed, and it was only 9:00 a.m. I tried to keep focused, an absurd attempt given what had occurred over the past twenty-four hours. It didn't help that Jules was relentlessly texting me her thoughts about it all. I could feel her panicked state as she continued to text, saying she couldn't stop thinking about me, that she was questioning her marriage among other things.

I got up from my desk to take a walk because I couldn't process what was happening. I took a seat in the front lobby to read and reread the messages. She was saying how confused she was, how she loved her husband yet in all the years they were together, she had never felt the way she did the night before with me. I didn't know how to respond. I had no interest in being with a woman, nor did I care to be in a relationship at all. I couldn't fathom the fact that sex could be so powerful, that it could cause someone to become so instantly possessed. I had never even done the things I did before that night, nor had I ever been more motivated to act in such vulgar vengeance. As I was reading, another message came through: "I can't get you out of my head! You're the devil disguised as a Jesus-loving lesbian."

With peace and gratitude,
Chole

Justified Vengeance

Dear Addie, may this note find you well.

That statement ceased all thought. I literally could not comprehend being associated with either of those labels. Intimacy, as far as I understood it, was between a man and a woman. Anything else was not actually intercourse or fornication, anatomically substantiated. In addition, for there to have been any devious charges of coveting, I would have had to sleep with her husband. I hadn't even allowed her to touch me, let alone him; therefore, I considered what I had done to be completely objective and nonbinary. I knew anatomy, what areas of the body become highly stimulated when softly touched. I knew how to read emotions, how to exchange people's sense of physical and mental insecurities with value and approval. And I knew from experience how sloppy men were at navigating a woman's body—furthermore, how much they undervalued fulfilling emotional hunger equally to the physical. Men had no attention to detail, no caress or intent to please another more than themselves. They approached intimacy with pitiful eyes and abbreviated ambition, flattering themselves with short performances as if such lame stamina also appeased their partner. It was coming together in my mind slowly yet ever so clearly. I had been searching for a way to capitalize on seduction without compromising my own body, and this couldn't have been a more obvious answer: destroy man's credibility by means of emasculation. I wasn't getting acknowledged or respected by exceeding them at work, so I had to hit them where it hurt most. Not only would I continue to outperform them at work, but I would now also eclipse their performance with the women they so pitifully wanted.

While Jules continued to text about her feelings and how to make sense of further engagement that was all I could think about. Obviously, I couldn't tell her that. I had no interest in being with a man or a woman, impartiality that made my mission all too easy. She already thought I was more intelligent and more aggressive than he was, and now I had stolen the one area he thought for sure only a man could succeed at. I'd be lying if I said I wasn't afraid of the thoughts invading my mind at the time. I had tried something unspeakable and found unexpected proficiency in it. Text messages continued to penetrate my cellular space faster than I could respond. The incessant barrage chartered an emotional current that could be felt ninety miles away. I didn't know how to respond to a woman telling me that I had caused her whole body to tremble in ecstasy. I had never experienced such interaction before and was too engrossed in the competing excitement for power to comprehend her feelings. My mind fell instantly inattentive to anything else, while my heart grew riddled with mild conviction and confusion. My adulterated appetite aligned perfectly with the tactics I needed to dominate in a cutthroat patriarchal world. I could get close enough to men in the sexual arena to feed off of the same power source without getting too close to compromise myself personally. It made perfect and logical sense in my mind.

At the same time, my heart was throwing out signals of treacherous danger, without explaining why. I was convinced that I was innocent against any wrongdoing since everyone involved was consenting. I literally could not discern why my heart was so distressed. I think that's the problem with matters of the heart: feelings are not facts. My heart's reluctance was loud enough to acknowledge yet impractical enough to silence. I wanted to be a symbol of love, yet I also wanted freedom to rebel in retribution to everything and everyone who attempted to hold me down. I had had enough of working so strenuously for inequitable recognition, and for being labeled lonely for wanting to be single, so much so that I thought the only road to obtaining respect was by way of force. After some time had passed and I didn't die, meaning I wasn't struck dead for any sins I may have committed, I interpreted God's lack of immediate punishment to be a green light to proceed. Under the influence of propitious power, I responded, telling her that I could come back down the following weekend.

It was hard to put a name or a label on what we were doing, mainly because for the first few months, it was a secret. Well, at least for me it was. I changed my name on social media accounts to a fictitious character so that I could maintain autonomy in my professional life. I disappeared from meetings and social events in what felt like covert operations where invisibility was the key to success. My calendar was filled with bogus bookings to afford the ability to withdraw from all forms of communication for hours at a time, strategically planning exactly how I could be missing in action without anyone actually noticing that I was. Then there was the plotting of entering and exiting her house. Given her home was literally connected to my parents' and down the street from my sister's, we had to ascertain a meetup in the next town. Once I solidified a discreet location, she would drive over to meet me. I would hop in the back seat of her car and lie down until we reached her back door, where I would then drape a jacket over my head in an attempt to be unrecognizable as I rushed in. By its very nature, an affair of any type is a disruption of routine and structure. There is no time spent in reality or everyday life tasks; it's all an illusion. A world created purely for fulfillment of the flesh, free from the stressors of traditional relational responsibility and accountability. It's a world that thrives on intensifying pleasure and blocking out pain. A world that welcomes fugitives desperate to rebel against any and all favor of discipline and obedience. When you look at it that way, it's not ironic to notice how the characteristics between an affair and a rebellion are essentially the same. They both aim to deliberately resist reverence for rules and order, and they both enable self-determined definitions of right and wrong.

Whatever it was lasted for the better part of a year. Over that period of time, we formed a bond that was as equally satisfying as it was terrifying. We took on the form of a couple in courtship, even though I thought she was using me just like I was using her. Turned out that wasn't the case, though; she developed feelings that I simply didn't know what to do with. I'd be a hypocrite if I didn't admit to appreciating her affection in an intimate friendship sort of way. Back then, every time my phone rang or text messages came through, it was either for work or for a family chore, meaning people only reached out to me when they needed something. It was refreshing for someone to be interested in me, for someone to simply care to ask how I was doing or how my day went. Our togetherness organically evolved beyond physical intimacy. Some nights, we would just hang out, she would softly rub my back, and we'd talk about life. It was nurturing in the most unordinary of ways. She enjoyed making playful fun of everything about me, particularly her take on my infatuation with money and appearances. She hated the Christian fish symbol I had on the back of my car, often avoiding being my passenger because of the hypocrisy it represented in the setting. Her honesty was authentic and exhilarating, so vastly different from the superficial world I was a slave to.

Given the distance, in addition to my travel schedule, it got harder to keep making the three-hour drive south. The more time I spent away, the more she wanted to know my every move, everywhere I had plans to go and everyone I intended to meet. If I didn't answer text messages quick enough, she would call nonstop until I answered. The few weekends I did make it back home, she capitalized on any opportunity to make a scene in front of family and friends, professing her love and insisting on their acceptance of me. Because I didn't refute it, I was labeled. Everyone, including my grandparents, knew I was having an affair with a married woman. I didn't care what anyone thought, nor did I care to rebuke the identity accusations. Her possessive nature was the bloodline to my purpose. My vested interest was in crushing my family's ideas for my life. Even when I wasn't home, she was. She lived next door, and they had to see her every single day—which meant every single day, she was a reminder to them that their ideas for my life were fruitless. Plus, as long as she was obsessing over me, she wasn't acknowledging her husband. I didn't even have to be physically present to be in her head. On numerous occasions, she told me that she had to picture me in order to be with him—it didn't get much more gratifying than that. It was all working together just as I had planned. My extended family stopped pressuring me about my dating life and why I wasn't married yet. I built that wall for protection, which allowed me to forget how worthless I was without a normal life trajectory. Against the sails of vindictive gains, there was a sense of overtness that began to open my eyes to the treachery my heart previously tried to warn me about.

Jealousy and paranoia quickly replaced even the slightest sense of enjoyment between Jules and me, from which point I wanted out. I didn't know how to end things amicably, which was critical given the close proximity to my family's home. The last thing I wanted to do was hurt her, which I'm sure sounds preposterous. A part of me felt an obligation to commit to something with her, whatever that even meant, in an undesirable attempt to hold myself accountable for my part in it all. I had capitalized on her desires and used her feelings as footholds for avengement that had nothing to do with her. I even started to feel guilty about what I had done to her husband. One of the last nights I stayed at her house, I caught a glimpse of him, in what felt like a slow-motion scene, uttering to one of his friends, "She has never looked at me that way." That should have dampened my ability to enjoy his defeat. Then I recalled his desperate flirting with me and other women and her relentless work to improve herself and their lives. Those thoughts quickly justified an ugly lack of compassion. I just wanted to disappear. I didn't want to talk about it anymore, I didn't want to say goodbye, I just wanted out. I did love her, very much so, just not with the impaired vision of romantic love the world is bound by. I loved how lost she was and how she didn't judge me for being equally so. I disregarded all attempts to discuss the future of the relationship, hoping it would just somehow go away on its own. My skin crawled for a distraction as I buried the remorse and focused on upping the game.

There are certain animals in the wild that are considered ambush predators. Their strategy is to hide in plain sight, camouflaging themselves with their surroundings, until their prey comes within striking distance. And when they strike, it is over before it began, the prey consumed before a struggle could even be considered. One could say I took a similar approach to life at that point. I changed my wardrobe and my appearance. While cutting my hair short was an unspoken confirmation to the rest of the world that the rumors about my sexuality were true, for me, it was more about fitting the look. Short hair was bold. Bold paired perfectly with lower-cut, button-down tops, form-fitting suit pants, and three-inch stilettos. I grew obsessed with looking perfect. Not one hair on my head could be out of place. My nails had to be manicured with an elegant beige polish, and my eye makeup had to be so impeccable it caused women to enviously question if my lashes were real. My clothes were precisely pressed and primarily navy blue and black: colors that denoted trust, elegance, authority, and power. My heels were aggressively pointed, my car was detailed weekly, my home was spotless, my speech and posture were well poised, and my work was consistently faultless. I read books and took courses on etiquette to further master the veil of superiority. It wasn't all about being better or being more put together than others, though there was certainly a strong undercurrent of that. Perfection to that extent drew on people's deepest levels of curiosity, both men and women. They needed to find flaws, and in order to do that, they had to get close. Like I said, ambush predator.

A few took the bait, then didn't know what hit them. I had never even made eye contact with them prior. Instead, I acquired credibility with all of the people around them, in particular, the men who unabashedly wanted them. That was the target, women desperate for a good man in a sea of smug ones. By the time they engaged with me personally, one conversation would affirm I already had them. They happened to be leading conduits in cross-functional departments I needed to succeed at my work. Needless to say, thereafter, any request I had was instantly prioritized and responded to with a greater sense of urgency than shown anyone else, including male managers. Tangible proof that men weren't the only ones with sensual power and influence. I received two dozen red roses after one rendezvous with a card that read, "You're good." I caught people peeking at that arrangement on my desk for days, eager to know something about the mysterious delivery. Obscurity was what made the camouflage so effective. I posted a picture of the roses online, subconsciously hoping Jules would see and get so angry she'd end things. Inadvertently, it was like throwing fuel on a fire. After receiving a number of impassioned phone calls, in addition to public displays of contempt, her disdain for me was finally achieved. Deep down, she knew I wasn't in it for the same reasons she was, and the fact that I was too cowardly to admit it ate at me. I cried for a few days, prayed a little too. It had been a while since I talked to God, since going to church during that time made me feel ashamed and dirty. So I hid, with pictures of her and me, pleading for God to give her happiness and somehow let love conquer it all. I was relieved she stayed with her husband and moved on. Literally too. Not long after that, they moved away from the neighborhood. Jealousy was her gasoline. Pain was mine.

I never could explain some of the strange things that I noticed at work after those encounters. Women started dressing like me, cutting their hair short, and trying to imitate my work style. I thought I was hallucinating until someone I did not know approached me in the bathroom one day and said, "Imitation is the highest form of flattery, eh?" There was a serious stalker as well. She would mail gifts to my home and leave lengthy notes on my desk, closing each with how much she wanted to be like me. I was always scared that she would be hiding in the bushes, waiting for me when I got home from extended work trips. I considered filing a harassment complaint with HR; however, I saw how those things went with men. The complaint was heard because it legally had to be, then never acted on. Worse yet, many times, the tables would turn, and the victim would be blamed for the offender's behavior. Being the master of avoidance that I was, I managed to keep the threat at bay by not acknowledging it existed.

During my annual performance review that year, I expected another promotion. I had been promoted the year before to the title I originally applied for and had since made exponential strides in demonstrating practical application of the knowledge I had gained. I expected to be acknowledged for that, for the relationships I had built with customers that led to higher sales and increased brand loyalty. Yet my boss didn't endorse any of that. Instead, he told me that I would never grow in the organization if I didn't start selling myself. He told me how difficult it was to be promoted, implying because of my gender, and that in order to get recognized, I had to have a brag pitch prepared for any time I found myself in the presence of an executive. Clearly, I could be a lot of things; a gloat was not one of them. If there was anything sacred left about me, it was my work ethic. I asked him what would happen if I refused to sell myself, to which he replied, confirming that I would not ever be acknowledged for the value and integrity of my work alone. I refused to do that and instantly made up my mind to leave. I started to network and landed an interview with another company without much effort at all. Turned out, what that first recruiter said about working at this company and the access it would open to the industry was right. My credentials paired with the company name provided all the negotiating power I needed to leave within a month's time of that conversation.

Shortly after submitting my resignation, I came to find that my stalker had caught wind of my departure and used her graphic design talents to create a life-size poster of me for everyone to sign. It was a strangely suitable end to that turbulent chapter of my life. In a matter of three years, I had begun a career that felt more like purpose than it ever did work, purchased a home, gotten a DWI, lost essential privileges of daily life, watched my grandfather die, witnessed my sister get married, had an affair with a married woman, and transformed into a promiscuous corporate assassin. I carried that and a semblance of mixed feelings with me in my hurry to get out, along with a life-size companion of myself.

With peace and gratitude,
Chole

Control

Dear Addie, may this note find you well.

I came across that poster almost a decade later, when we had to pack up the home I grew up in. My family kept it as a joke. I gave them one last laugh, then put it out with the garbage. I sometimes catch myself thinking back on those days, wondering what people thought about me. The industry was so small that I eventually heard rumors of what was said, nothing anyone had fact to base on though. I sought dominance and manifested it into my identity. Hard to expect anyone to find me approachable, or likable, for that matter. Dominance was literally my greatest strength, and several behavioral aptitude tests further proved as such. I fit the definition in the most unbalanced of ways. I competed regardless of cost. I detested inaction so much that I stomped over people to get things done. I accepted challenges and achieved results in areas nobody else would even try at. I was commanding and outspoken, and I questioned everything and everyone. I was resolute with zero patience or humility, petrified of ever being vulnerable and taken advantage of. I knew my behavior was turning darker than I had ever imagined it could, yet I could not see another possible way to survive. I started talking to God again before starting the new job, praying for his will to be done. Assuming his will would show up like a delightful intervention that required no action from me whatsoever. I even considered applying to nursing school, thinking that I could leverage my knowledge from the medical side of business to serve others in a purer sense. Student loan debt killed that thought rather quickly though. The new position came with a 25 percent increase in pay, which promised more practicality in the face of financial debt than any good intention. Despite the fact that my greatest defense mechanisms were control and isolation, I had a desire deep in the depths of my heart for love to conquer it all. That's why I got that tattoo on my hip, *Omni a Vincit Amor*—Love Conquers All—in Latin. It was a permanent testament to everything I wanted to embody yet didn't know how to obtain. Maybe not so ironic that that was around the time I met you.

I approached the new job as an opportunity to recalibrate, revisit who I wanted to be and what I wanted to be known for. It was a smaller company that promised to promote on the merit of work achievements and professionalism. Furthermore, I was offered opportunities to lead the highest-profile development projects, as well as drive one of the most clinically successful procedures outside of the United States into the country. It was the chance to take my experience to a global level, to really prove my value and worth. I had never been to Europe before that, nor did I even have a passport. I spent the first week working to expedite one and the second in a crash course on the state of the business over there. The company's strategy for growth was by means of acquisition, which was especially awfully managed on a customer level. The products that drove the revenue in my division were acquired overseas, and due to poor relationship management, they were on the verge of losing their principal customer and clinical advocate. Up to that point, my boss was managing all customer relationships; needless to say, it wasn't going well. It felt like the perfect season to start exchanging duplicity for honesty. I even decorated my cube walls with popular scripture verses in hopes it would keep me accountable to the good person I really wanted to be.

A few days before I left for Europe, I met you in the city to meet your best friend. I wore camouflage of purity and virtue in an effort to hide my corruption. I wanted so desperately for you to like and respect me that I didn't share a single thing about myself with you, other than work. I was strategically agreeable to every other topic that was brought up and pretended to be innocent to the rest. I didn't drink, didn't stay up late, didn't have sex, didn't go to clubs, didn't have debt, and my family was absolutely not dysfunctional. Even though none of that was true, I didn't want to admit I was associated with anything that could be even remotely related to an imperfect person. I took full control of the impression I wanted you to have of me. All you needed to know was that I was ambitious, wealthy, kind, generous, and charming. Just writing that out makes me realize how unquestionably lifeless that sounds. Obviously, I could not see that at the time. There was just something very different about you. From the first time I met you at that sushi restaurant, I knew you were going to have a profound impact on my life. I had to seek the meaning of that notion because nothing in my entire life had ever been so undoubtedly clear.

Things seemed to have gone well that day in the city. I felt like a little kid in kindergarten who had just made a new best friend, but I never told you that, out of fear I would appear desperate or needy. There was something so familiar about you, something safely relatable that prompted choice. I chose for you to be in my life. I chose for you to be my friend. That was the first time I actually made a relationship choice. How do you tell someone that? Up to that point, I just accepted whoever showed up in my life; I didn't put much thought into how their life could influence mine, for better or worse. So, I'm sure now you can begin to imagine how deeply it hurt when you completely stopped all communication after that day in the city. We had been talking for a few months up until then, up until I decided I wanted to let you into my life. Then, not even so much as a goodbye or a reason why.

I arrived in Europe the day after that, riding planes, trains, and taxicabs to my destination through the most beautiful landscapes I had ever seen. I remember looking out of the train window around the Swiss Alps at one point, seeing people parasailing, soaring freely through the air, and wondering how I could be so sad in the presence of such breathtaking sights. Since my reign of dominance began, I had never been rejected by anyone, nor had I had to chase anyone. I was chased. I was desperately sought after by men and women alike. Then there you were, playing a similarly charming game to mine, allowing me to think you were someone I could trust, without so much as an ounce of remorse about it. That first time you walked away made me feel so exposed and betrayed. It was a serious step, to consider allowing someone to be my friend, only to have them disregard the precious vulnerability that takes like a crumpled-up paper ball. Even with all of that hurt, and despite rational judgment, everything inside of me said you were different. So much so that despite the hurt feelings and heavy heart, I still chose you.

When I wasn't invested in work on that trip, I was thinking of what I had done for you to abandon me the way you did. This was the first time in a while I felt like I actually had something to lose, and I was obsessed with figuring out what that was. In the process of trying to be a better person, there were things I carried and things I tried really hard to leave behind. Being new to the organization, coming from the preeminent company in the industry, and placed in an influential position did not make for instant allies, especially outside of the States. Almost immediately, I could tell who was talking to me in an effort to butter me up and who wanted to get close because that's what you do with your rivals. I was hopeful I had escaped a savage landscape in exchange for a more even playing field, and I had even renounced the use of seduction and destruction going forward. I wanted honest companionship, moreover friendship that didn't demand me to compromise anything about myself. Over the course of those first few weeks in Europe, I remember sending you pictures of the foods I was eating and places I had been. You always said you wanted to go to Italy; I guess I thought, if nothing else, you could live vicariously through my experience until you got there yourself. It was refreshing to finally get a reply from you. I thought to ask why you had finally responded after cutting off all communication, but I didn't want to risk stirring up conflict and scare you off again.

In my spare time, I rode the public transit system to explore various parts of Switzerland, France, and Italy. I was particularly attracted to churches and the architecture that seemed to bring what I knew about the Bible into modern-day life. The statues and depictions of Jesus provoked my heart with wonder. The statue of Mary holding Jesus's body in the Trinita dei Monti was particularly mesmerizing. I stared at it for some time, with only one thought steadily on my mind, *Who is this man who died like this ... for me?* Everything about that trip took on meaning. The days I spent working were equally profound to the days I spent exploring. When the time had come for me to head home, a woman from the office in France offered to ride with me to the airport to make sure I arrived okay. It was a quiet ride since she didn't speak English very well. I tried asking her questions about how she liked her work and how she felt about some of the changes taking place. Small talk to build up to what I really wanted to ask her. We were just about to the airport when I got up the courage to see if she believed in Jesus. She responded, "Yes, yes," with a humble smile. I was cutting it close on time to get to my plane, so I did not have the chance to ask her anything more about it. As I flew above the clouds that night, I wondered why God created it all. I never questioned *if* he did; belief in the fact that God was the Creator of the world was the only belief I had that actually aligned with anything the Bible said. I just couldn't help but wonder what the purpose of the world was, with sadness and loneliness growing to become my two most trusted companions.

I spent the following months completely immersed in work. I was in surgeries again on a weekly basis, this time for research in new product development. I loved learning new anatomy, the deficiencies with current treatment options, and working with surgeons to develop ideas that could better improve outcomes and ultimately patient lives. I was closer to patients in that role, often accompanying design surgeons on rounds to hear firsthand what kind of pain patients presented with and the impact it had on their daily lives. It brought what I did to life in a new way. In my previous role, I did a lot of work in the operating room, but I never heard from the patient before or after regarding their experience. I discovered a passion for voice of customer feedback and using that feedback to develop technical instructions for engineers to implement into their designs. I was making another niche role for myself, as nobody else was thinking about product development from such a holistic perspective. For me, solutions had to satisfy all customers, not just one. Customers in my case included surgeons and patients, of course, but also manufacturers and sales representatives. I didn't consider design solutions to be good if procuring them was impossible or if adoption forced change. It was a beautiful challenge to me, to figure out how to serve everyone involved. The work came so naturally that it caught me off guard. Some days, I didn't feel like I deserved the amount of money I was making because it was so easy and enjoyable. Other days, I felt like I deserved a lot more money because of the amount of time I was spending each day working. I was glad to be seeing you again, even if it was just once in a while for a cup of tea and stroll through the bookstore. Every time you asked me to hang out, I felt like I had won the lottery. I considered the fact that maybe you came back into my life because you had taken pity on me after all the emails I sent while in Europe. And maybe that was true; it was certainly always in the back of my mind, which made it difficult for me to really trust you after that. I made a new friend at work, Leocadia, who brought a welcome distraction to my constant thoughts of you. I called her Lee, and she was like a breeze of reprieve that blew in out of nowhere.

I met her a few weeks after you stopped talking to me again. That was the second time you said you needed space, which just added to the confusion, because I couldn't figure out how you could need space from a casual friend you had tea with every few weeks. Anyway, her first day was during a sales training I was leading. When she walked into the education center, I saw every man's head swivel to watch her go by. I always told her that her body didn't match her personality. She was of Spanish descent, with unblemished olive skin, long, beautiful black hair, and a curvy shape that clearly made men drool. She passed them all up and sat down next to me. As I observed her reaction to the indirect attention, I noticed she had an engagement ring on. The first thought that entered my mind was that she was in my world now, which meant that ring wouldn't stay on for long. Bad habits die hard. She was not the serious corporate type I was used to. She was laid back, hilarious, and sporadic. She also loved food as much as I did, making her all around genuinely authentic and incredibly refreshing to be around. She had a problem, though, that most people hadn't a clue about: she was a sex addict. I picked up on that from our very first conversation. I felt safe with her flaws, maybe because I could see myself in them. It made me feel less alone, in a similar darkness that threatened my light on a daily basis. As time went on, we spent just about all day, every day together. We talked before and after work, usually about the day or other random nonsense. She understood work drama and was probably the most enjoyable person I had ever known. I craved alone time, especially after spending eight hours a day in meetings. For whatever reason, I didn't mind talking to her more after work; I didn't ever get sick of her company. I think she was my first real friend, and of course, not by choice this time but by chance. The distinct difference in my relationship with you and my relationship with Lee consequently had me strenuously doubting my ability to discern choices in my life. Without any sort of intimacy, we grew close. The ring eventually disappeared too, as I predicted.

About a year later, our boss came to me, asking what I thought about mentoring her. He said he wanted her to report to me as a preface to an upcoming promotion as well as to give her the focused training she needed. It was a roundabout way of admitting he was not giving her the attention she needed despite it being his responsibility. I couldn't understand how he managed to keep his job. He knew nothing about the products, was terrible at building relationships with customers, was anxiety-ridden all of the time, and used me as a dumping ground for the issues he should have had the ability to deal with. He was especially oblivious to the challenges I had in the industry as a woman. Of the countless inappropriate encounters I would end up experiencing at that company, I brought him the one I was sure he would have been able to help with. I regret ever thinking that was a good idea. I had been working with the chief of surgery at a highly accredited hospital to author a competitive cadaveric study to evaluate the clinical efficacy of two different treatment options for more challenging anatomic deformities. I was extremely passionate about that project and the outcome it promised in helping surgeons choose the best treatment option according to patient need. When the surgeon finished the study, we met to discuss it at a hotel bar during a mutual work trip. After some small talk, he went to pull a copy of the abstract from his blazer pocket. He placed it on the bar and proceeded to slide it toward me, noticeably never releasing the paper from his control. I didn't pick up on that until later because, in the moment, all I remember was feeling so proud and excited to read it. As I went to grab it, he slid it back toward himself, saying, "You know what comes next, sweetheart." Caught off guard, I replied, "No, actually, I don't." He folded up the abstract and put it back into his blazer pocket, exchanging it for his hotel room key. I couldn't believe what was happening. He was blackmailing me for work, a sexual favor in exchange for my study. It was far from the first time I had been intimidated by a sexual advance with work; however, it was the first time with something I cared about so deeply on the line. To buy myself some time, I told him I had another meeting to go to and would have to revisit his offer the following night. I ran to report the incident to my boss, who literally scoffed in disbelief prior to saying, "I think you may have misunderstood him; I cannot see him doing that to you."

I can confidently say that the best thing my boss was good at was victimizing victims. I left his helpless presence and went further up the chain to the division president. Right before he could insinuate the same, I invited him to the same bar the following night. I asked him to position himself in such a way that his back was toward me so when the surgeon arrived, he would be unrecognizable. I wore my best-looking black suit with a low-cut button-down and three-inch heels, ordered a glass of wine, and waited for my company to arrive. I smiled and acted as if I were happy to see him, despite the sour temptation to vomit in my mouth. I asked him to show me the abstract once more and remind me of what he wanted in exchange for it, as if I was eager to hear his vulgar desires. Mind you, he had a wife of thirty-plus years at home and children beyond college age. With his mouth watering like a man lost in the desert about to get a drink, he spoke his obscene wishes just loud enough for the president to hear. I stood up, tapped his shoulder, and said, "Was that clear enough for you?" then walked away with my head held high as the surgeon fell blindsided into a trap his own game had staged for him.

Another aspect about Lee that I appreciated was her understanding for what we dealt with as women in that industry. She knew what it was like to be looked at like an object and spoken to like a perpetual subordinate. She understood the level of sexual intimidation that threatened the purpose in our daily lives. She was the first person who I felt like I could really relate to about almost anything, including God. We would take rides to get coffee or escape office drama at a nearby lakeside park. We vented about the things out of our control and pondered God's opinion on it all. It was the most innocent companionship I had ever had; it couldn't have felt more natural. That's why I neglected to talk much about my relationship with her to you. Every time I mentioned Lee's name, you became visibly uncomfortable. I never could figure out why, though, given you and I could not even seem to figure out how to be authentic acquaintances, let alone friends. I wanted what I had with her, with you. I guess I thought talking about my relationship with Lee would help you see that I was a real person, worthy of genuine friendship. I always blamed myself for whatever lacked between us, which is why I guess a small part of me wanted you to be jealous. I wanted you to appreciate me the way she did. I wanted you to see value in me as a person the way she did. I wanted to share deep life questions and random thoughts with you the way I did with her. But every effort I made to do that with you, you never seemed to have the time. You wanted me in your life yet didn't want to invest the time to really have me there. Then you got upset when I grew closer to someone else. You were hard to figure out, my dear. And even still, I loved you anyway.

Lee was a good person, a truly gorgeous soul. The only regret I have is allowing my boss to change what we had when he made her report to me. Our whole dynamic changed. I also felt like it was inappropriate to hang out the way we were now that I was responsible for her supervision at work. I tried to draw a line in our bond, especially when joking around in meetings and around other colleagues, to avoid disrespecting the role I was given. Seemed like the harder I tried to do that, the more intense she became at trying to get closer. When I would call her over to my desk to ask her a question, she would approach with a smirk on her face, then prop herself up on my desk with her legs crossed. I tried not to think too far into it, but something started to feel different about her demeanor toward me. It solidified my concerns when she stopped calling me as much after-hours. Her communication outside of work shifted from playful banter to selfies of herself while she was out with her guy of the month. Except the guy was never in the picture, nor was her face. I never knew how to respond without offending her with my disinterest in what she was trying to show me. I would reply with a smiley face or a comment on her surroundings, like, "Wow, look at that beach," in reply to a selfie of her in a bathing suit. Or, "How's the food?" to a selfie of her chest in a restaurant. I was growing nervous and sick to my stomach as I attempted to grasp what was happening. Or rather yet, what I was rapidly losing.

I didn't have those types of feelings for her, in addition to the fact that I had become emotionally attached to her as my only trusted partner in daily life. Once again, innocent companionship just could not exist. I didn't want to ask if she was flirting with me, out of fear of messing up what was left of our friendship by potentially having misread her advances. I did my best to deflect, until I couldn't. We had been assigned to colead a training together for the sales organization, which was prefaced by a late night of preparation the day prior. We ordered takeout to the office as we worked through dry runs of each presentation. We had invited a surgeon to present on the first day, who showed up late to review his part. The meeting ran until close to ten o'clock at night, leaving just the three of us at the office. I was exhausted and frustrated, disarranging my hair as the conversation dragged on. Suddenly, I felt Lee's foot slowly crawl up my leg as she smiled and said to the surgeon, "That's what she must look like in bed." I closed my laptop and called it a night, while they laughed and told me to relax. I was sure the next day was going to be awkward.

When I arrived, half of the class—all men, of course—was

standing around Lee. She was sitting down, and they were standing around her in a half-circle form. I saw that and felt a surge run through my veins, an irrefutable sensation to devour. If she wanted to play this game, I was going to beat her at it. With each step I took toward the small crowd, I heard a faint voice telling me not to do it, to reject the intense desire for dominance and control. It felt like I literally had two souls, a devious evil one and a virtuous good one, fighting against each other for authority. I noticed three of the men talking to her were wearing wedding rings, with their tongues practically wagging as they spoke. That solidified which side I chose to feed. I slipped between them subtly when she suddenly dropped her pen on the floor. I winked at her, squatted down in my stiletto heels, picked up the pen, and gently caressed the back of her calf as I lifted it from the ground to hand it to her. She surely didn't see that coming, as she looked back at me practically melting in her chair. I walked away and started the training with total control of that room. It is very difficult to kill ambush prey, especially in the wayward wild.

With peace and gratitude,
Chole

Pride

Dear Addie, may this note find you well.

There was a deeper part of me that truly wanted to change. Yet no matter how hard I tried or how many certifications I completed, change for the better was perpetually unreachable. I had been on a roller coaster of emotions for years. The normalcy of that began to blanket my body with a familiar sense of sadness. I was reaching a level of heartache that subtly transformed day by day into hopelessness. The harder I tried to convince everyone else that I was happily in control of my life, the more imprisoned I felt by overpowering confusion between my head and my heart. My heart told me that loving people meant pleasing them, while my head told me that loving myself meant rebelling against people. When I tried to please people, I didn't like who I became. When I rebelled against people, I despised who they were. Peace and genuine happiness grew further and further from my grasp the harder I tried to generate it. Every single day, the path I walked felt like it was going to buckle underneath me. If my emotions had a forecast, they would have predicted a daily threat of despondent disturbance with an accumulation of disoriented delusion. I craved stability while I forged uncertainty, results derived from the promises of ungoverned behavior and the immature inability to firmly say yes or no in any given situation. Saying no was persistently prefaced with anxiety and the notion of disappointment. If I said no, I felt like I was letting someone down, which I never wanted to do since I knew how rotten that felt. On the other hand, saying yes felt equally as damaging since it always took something from me. Somewhere along the way, my desire to see people happy became intertwined with my deep and desperate desire for acceptance and approval. Changing who I was to please another never brought the kind of acceptance and approval I sought. Just like rebelling in forceful attempts to make people accept me never brought the kind of acceptance and approval I desperately desired. Yet I continued to try anyway.

My first attempt at setting boundaries was with Lee, ensuring she knew that the flirtatious teasing between us could not go beyond just that. It was impossible to ignore the connection between us, but I was still her boss, after all. When we were together in meetings that would have otherwise been prime grounds for intimidating persuasion, our allegiance came to build a sort of force field around us. Women thought we were the best and closest of friends, while men felt highly intoxicated at the thought of us together. Both sides kept a peaceable distance. Women didn't try to fake relationships, and men knew they didn't have a chance in the world. Despite the fact that my discomfort with deception was growing, the fact that my connection with women was like a repellent to distasteful men made the moral compromise worth it. The power in that was like physical armor for me, a dependable emotional safety net. Having an ally and confidant in this war was more than I ever could have asked for, and more comforting than anything I ever knew I needed. I had been building an isolating wall around myself for so long—defending against intimidating notions, discouraging conclusions, and vulgar advances—that I had never allowed myself to know what it would be like to have a companion in the cause.

It was always comical to hear people say how smart I must have been to be in the line of work that I was. You used to say the same thing. Whenever you introduced me to a new friend or a colleague at your work events, you would emphasize my work in association with my identity. I never enjoyed that. Maybe because I never felt like my career was intellectually difficult. If I succeeded at any aspect of it, it was because of fortitude and a persistent will to work hard. That wasn't something you learned in school or earned from high exam scores. No, the most difficult part was navigating the toxic cultural tides of greed, lust, pride, and envy. To say it was mentally exhausting almost feels like an understatement, mainly because loneliness was the only rest my mind ever had. Being alone was the only time I felt safe. I was not emotionally safe at home or with extended family even still. My parents persistently focused on my flaws, particularly the fact that, as a woman, my life was preposterous without a husband and a family. My grandparents succeeded at making me feel like my career accomplishments were luck of the draw, as if every achievement I had was a shock because I was a woman succeeding in a man's world. My mom-mom was the only one who never made me feel less than human in my own skin. Whether she agreed with my behaviors and choices or not was never spoken. She occasionally asked questions and made me aware of having healthy boundaries, yet she never passed judgment. She did her best to love and accept me just as I was, and it would be years before I would realize the freedom that had provided for me to figure things out in a safe space.

Lee was the closest relationship I had to feeling the same kind of trust I did with my mom-mom. I wasn't able to trust a soul, which made it all the more devastating to accept the fact that our relationship was being slowly consumed by corruption, just like every other. To distract myself from mourning the loss of the pure idea of our friendship, I revived my focus on being perfect and making my colleagues feel incompetent at their jobs. Promoting the weaknesses of others to avoid facing my own was the only way I knew how to cope. I was no doubt insecure about opening myself up to someone, only to have my pure intentions corrupted by discouraging words or animalistic behavior. A fierce and unapproachable exterior felt like the safest guard against people in general. I started going out more at night too, extending my fraudulent flirting to gain access to exclusive clubs and all sorts of premieres around the city for magazines and events I knew nothing about. As the hurt deepened in my heart, I grew more angry with God and became determined to prove that pure intentions could not exist in this world. Since deceitful persuasion was reality and the actual way of getting ahead in this life, I was going to give myself to it. It just hurt too much to continue trying to do good only to meet deception in the end anyway. I further convinced myself that I had no need for a friend like Lee, or anyone else, for that matter. I felt like trusting another human with my emotions was as useful as any other means of self-sabotage. The thought of changing and being a better person took on new meaning. I started going to church again on Sundays and volunteered my time to worthy causes. Nevertheless, I gave up on trying to change myself since I had failed at every turn of that endeavor. People returned to being nothing more than pawns to me, sources of consumption to obtain what I wanted, in the game that was life. There wasn't much reason for me to be convinced otherwise.

I spent the better part of that year partying excessively on weekends, drinking heavily Friday and Saturday and hungover on Sunday. Drinking was another aspect of life I previously thought I had a handle on. You had stopped talking to me again, for no apparent reason, and I just couldn't trust Lee anymore to be a source of safe friendship without adding to the changing intentions there. With no one left to trust, I felt an overwhelming sense to run and hide. I didn't know anything other than hiding in an obnoxious persona to avoid being exposed for how sad I really was. And drinking, which I hated, happened to be the best coverup. I guess I wasn't really satisfied with the results of my behavior; I just didn't know of another way to deal with life and people. I felt like my weaknesses were excelling faster than any good characteristic I potentially had to offer. Every choice I made, every decision that promised peace, control, and stability, were feeling more like emotional traps. I remembered how you said that you loved me and that whenever I needed you, you would be there. Well, I needed you then, and you were furthest from being there for me. When I called, you never picked up. When I texted, you responded hours later, only to kindly brush me off. No one's words ever made me feel so connected to them as yours did. And no one's actions ever made me feel as unwanted or alone as yours did.

Emma was the only person left who I socialized with outside of my family and work. I trusted her with some things but not all things. There was always a lingering feeling in the background of our friendship that made me feel like she wanted more from me. More that I could not give. So, I avoided getting too close in order to avoid sending the wrong message. She liked to hang out in an area of the city called the gayborhood, which for the most part made me feel really uncomfortable. As time went on and the more time we spent there, I could at least see the novelty in the broad sense of acceptance in those places. Nobody judged one another or cared how much money anyone made. There was nothing to prove; people thrived on being different, not on competing. That was a foreign concept to me. Anyhow, I remember catching a glimpse of you at a club we were at. A couple of hours after, you texted me to check in and tell me about the busy night you had ahead of you with work. I sent you a text the next day, asking how your work went and if you happened to be out in the city. You avoided directly answering by responding with an invitation to the upcoming annual Christmas festival on the other side of town. I envied your ability to lie so well. I was always such a bad liar.

By this point, I could detect the pattern: we were on again during fall and winter and off again during spring and summer. It was the fourth year of that routine, and I guess I will never know why that was. Maybe the holidays were especially tough for you, as they were for me. And maybe you needed someone to survive the season with, and I was equally reliable in never saying no to you. Either way, despite the fact that the on-and-off communication was a maddening push and pull on my heart, I took you up on any offer to meet. Abandonment and distrust were closer friends of mine than you ever were, and I suppose that's partially what made you comfortable. I could depend on not trusting people, and since you were so untrustworthy, I chose the devil I knew. At the same time, I had a desperate desire to figure out why I was so drawn to your companionship. We went to the festival together and barely talked, as if we were just two strangers with a past connection, dwelling once again in the same vicinity. I departed your company that day feeling exceptionally inept. I went out in the city with Emma the following night, on a mission. We were at a popular club, sitting at the bar people watching. I was doing a little more than that; I was scanning the room, doing a character assessment to gather who the players were and who the insecure types were.

You were a player, from what I gathered, so I figured the best way to better understand you was to get to know another player. Short of looking in a mirror, I shifted my attention to observe how the ones at that particular club operated. One girl caught my eye immediately. She owned the room and had power over all of the people in her orbit. She commanded respect, and you could tell that people knew they were either welcome or not in her presence. I had that kind of power at work, and I wanted it in my personal life. I wanted that kind of unspoken influence in society in general. Knowing I was way out of my league trying to talk to a real lesbian, I didn't move far from the bar for almost an hour. Emma had no idea what I was up to, because not even she knew the game I was playing. I told her I was interested in the girl in the back room and wanted to go talk to her. She got uncomfortably jealous and ditched me. Once again, my focus was on me and what I wanted. I used Emma so that I wouldn't have to go out alone. I had an idea of what I wanted to do but did not know how it would pan out. We had driven into the city together, and I didn't even give thought to how she was getting home once she left me. Nor did I understand why she would be jealous. I knew she had some kind of feelings for me, but I had never once allowed her to believe I was even remotely interested.

The name of the girl in the back room was Shae. She put up a front like she had zero interest in me, and I had no appetite for trying to flirt with her. I studied the setting a little longer and realized she was in the middle of something with a woman across the room. From afar, it looked like they were a couple, maybe fighting and out with mutual friends, clearly not together. I decided to capitalize on the vibe, walking over to Shae and asking, "Is that your girl over there?" She said, "She used to be." I asked her if she wanted to make her jealous, to which she quickly replied, "Maybe." I put my arm around her and asked her to walk out with me. I didn't know the person I was that night. It was like someone else took over my body and was using it to act out notions I would never or could never do. When we got outside,

I told her she could have full reign of my body. The only way I was going to adopt her kind of commanding power was to feel what she did to get that power, by experiencing it for myself. We went back to her place, where in the process of doing what we were doing, I was so disgusted that I gagged, clearly not drunkenly numb enough to do what my irrational mind had cooked up. Thankfully, Shae was more drunk than I was, so it didn't last long. I had learned what I needed to, gotten what I came for. It was her commanding presence that had power, surely not intimacy, from what I had just experienced. But maybe that was just because I had zero interest and was grossly turned off. Nevertheless, I was searching because rejection had me obsessively fixated on mastering the art of seduction for the sole purpose of no longer just being accepted—but being utterly undeniable. The problem with that was that the lure always caught a broader catch than the target. Shae would end up falling for me, well ... for an idea of me, which undoubtedly weighed heavy on my heart.

Shae and I became good friends, despite how I felt about a romantic relationship with her. I was truthful with her, to an extent. I never admitted that I was not attracted to women, but I didn't deny it either, because I actually enjoyed her company a lot once I got to know her. I enjoyed her companionship and thought if I told her the truth about my intentions, there was no way she would still be my friend. Despite befriending her in a lie, I felt more emotionally safe in her company than anyone else I knew at the time. I started hanging out with her every weekend and spent time getting to know her family too, who were equally as welcoming and exuded of a warm sense of belonging. For the most part, it was the same routine: we would go out to dinner and talk, then go out and drink for hours. Dinner was what I enjoyed the most, mainly because it was an opportunity for me to ask her questions about why she was with women and then her thoughts on God and what he thought about it. She grew up Catholic and had a lot of stories from her experience with religion. I would ask her what she thought about certain parts of the Bible, and she would challenge my doubts in her replies. I appreciated the fact that she didn't make fun of me for asking questions about God so often or asking what she thought God thought of some of the things we did. For the most part, everyone I spoke to believed God was an accepting and merciful God who loved humans just as we are, sins and all. There was a comforting sense of truth resonating from that; however, something also felt profoundly missing.

My life was beginning to feel like one giant scavenger hunt, with truth being the ultimate aim of my pursuit. I wondered what truth even was, moreover what made it so, if every word and promise I had come to know was destined to either elude or fail me in the end. I fought fear of rejection with stubborn arrogance, which promised power yet alternately welcomed drastic swings between pride and hopelessness into my mental state. I remember some days seeking reprieve in the lobby of the building I worked in. I would sit and watch the people who came to wash the windows. They looked so carefree using their tools to work their task, completing it without any sort of entanglement with drama, gossip, greed, or pride. It was simple, honest work. I watched those people day after day, growing more and more aware of the fact that I had no idea what I was doing anymore. I couldn't see the point to it anymore. I dove fiercely into the world in effort to find peace, happiness, and genuine joy. So far, all I was finding was my worst fears coming true: my parents and my family were right. Maybe I really was naive, with worthless passion. Too foolish to know how the world really worked and too idealistic to realize that the dreams I had for a better life were worthless.

I started spending hours at night after work in my bathtub, sipping wine by candlelight and delighting in the sound of utter nothingness each time I submerged. As I drifted slowly underwater into the quietude, I fantasized about the freedom in disappearing. Everyone wanted something from me, and nobody wanted me for me. I felt guilty for my parents' dissatisfaction in me. I wasn't living up to the expectations they had for my life; therefore, their unhappiness and discord were my fault. If I wasn't feeling guilty for that, I was feeling ashamed for disappointing everyone else's expectations for me as a woman. I was so tired. The kind of tired that you can't sleep off. Tired of fighting a standard that the world provided. Every time I came up for air, I came up with more reasons to die than live, with only one thought emerging, *How do I escape from this?* I was losing hope in the existence of genuine love and becoming more desperate to break free from the unceasing cycle of guilt and shame. I wondered, if I slipped under the water and just never came back up, would anyone even care? Probably not. Definitely not.

Lee introduced me to chakra meditation after I confided in her about my thoughts on the window washers. She left a note in my car after the first session that said, "Peace is not the absence of conflict, it's in the presence of God." How could I not love that? By the third session of weekly meditations, I had figured out how to let go and experience an escape of mind. By the fourth week, I fell into such a deep meditative state that I felt like my body floated a few inches off of the floor. The feeling was deeper and more freeing than any underwater immersion or long night of drinking had ever offered. I wanted more of it. I started meditating multiple times a week, and for a while, it was helping me find peace and calm. That was, until I inevitably had to face the people and circumstances that triggered unrest in my soul. So, Lee introduced me to another way of finding peace and calm, in the form of marijuana. She liked baking it into cupcakes, which I had never tried before. I didn't try smoking it in high school when everyone thought it was cool. I didn't try drugs at all, for that matter. She made it seem safe and harmless, so I indulged. Little did I know that eating it led to a much longer-lasting experience than I noticed others had after smoking. I was enchanted by it. It was even more mind-freeing than meditation. We had a blast eating marijuana muffins and listening to reggae music. We escaped reality for a few hours at a time—long enough to forget the pain and short enough to realize that it wasn't as much of an escape as it was a respite from reality.

Lee eventually confronted me about her feelings for me. I think you picked up on that, and maybe that was another reason you stopped talking to me, yet again. Either way, I told her I loved her as a friend and on top of that was her boss, so nothing could really happen in the way of a romantic relationship. I thought those were two solid reasons for maintaining autonomy without hurting her feelings with my lack of shared attraction. I never expected her to start searching out new job opportunities so that she could eliminate the boss-subordinate excuse. This was a woman who could have any man she wanted—and I'm pretty sure did—making a very intense advance to be with me. I couldn't understand it. I couldn't understand why she would want me in that way. I had been chased by men and proposed to more than once, yet never for being my true self. I was closest to living in my own skin around Lee, which made me wonder what she saw in me that didn't leave her disappointed like everyone else. I also wondered, perhaps more mournfully, why our friendship wasn't enough. She enjoyed her last few months at work to the fullest, running her foot up and down my leg under the table during meetings and flirting shamelessly in front of groups of men. I won't claim to have been innocent. Her attention fed my hunger for acceptance, and her lust fed my desire to be loved for exactly who I was—sins and all.

I had a career mentor at the time and ended up telling him about my relationship with her. I'll never forget his response. He looked me directly in the eyes and said, "What a waste of a woman you are." He laughed after he said it, following up his statement with how beautiful I was and how he could not believe I could waste that on another woman—one of those compliments that feel more like a backhanded slap across the face. Lee got the same kind of criticism, which in a strange way sparked an unexpected level of care for her in me. The fact that she was willing to be insulted for loving me was the most virtuous act anyone had ever shown me. At one point, we joked about quitting our jobs and starting a car service together, driving men to and from the airport in tight black suits and heels. We thought, why not profit off of man's pitiful desperation in lust? The hypocrisy, I know.

I kept deflecting her advances, until I couldn't. She started messaging me about all of the things she fantasized about doing with me. I would laugh to myself and always reply with, "Why?" She told me one morning at work that on her last day, she was going to take me in the elevator and kiss me all the way down. I couldn't help but laugh. I mean, I truly loved this girl like my best friend. Why did it have to go this way? And still, once again, I wondered, what did I have to lose? She was funny, I loved being around her, there was no trouble through it all. Maybe, since I had no agenda and wanted nothing from her, this would be different. Maybe it was okay to see where it went.

Confusion consumed my mind. I pictured her and I being best friends, conquering the world in rebellious fashion together. The idea of that, as always, was more appealing than the reality. Once again, I could not handle what I had gotten myself into, so I resorted to tactics that would sabotage the relationship for me—the cowardly absence of courage to tell the truth about how I felt, in fear of further abandonment and rejection. I had completely lost sight of what was right and what was wrong. Instead of attempting to confront the confusion, I ran from it, right into a bottle. And, of course, alcohol was served at places where I could get a lot of attention by behaving promiscuously. I could control people's desires by toying with them the same way mine felt they always were.

One night, I was out at the same club that always guaranteed that game to be available. The owner invited me into her office for a beer and to show me around. I couldn't even pretend to be impressed anymore. My ego had fed from that source too many times. I was feeling the same result with every person I talked to. I remember going to leave, making it halfway down the thin alleyway that ran beside the back entrance, when I felt a hand grab my shoulder. It was Shae, asking why I was so upset, pleading for me to stay and talk. She had seen that I was in tears when I walked out. I told her that I didn't want to do this anymore and pushed her away. She thought I meant I didn't want to be out that night. What I really meant was that I didn't want my life anymore.

It was after midnight at that point. I cried tears of defeat the whole way home, wondering how God could allow me to exist in such a deeply disillusioned state. I was on the highway about three miles from my parents', approaching the exit for their house, when I noticed an SUV in my rearview mirror appearing to be speeding directly toward me. A matter of seconds later, I was hit, and the impact sent my car spinning down the highway. My car spun a few times before engaging with a cement guardrail, when the rear of my car was struck a second time by the same driver. I must have blacked out for a moment because the only thing I remember after the impact was my door opening and two strong hands pulling me out by my shirt; a couple driving the same way had witnessed the whole thing. Their rescue occurred right before my engine exploded into smoke. I remember struggling to stand up as they helped me gather myself. I asked them why they saved me, why they thought I was worth the risk of stopping in their path to pluck me from that place. They didn't answer, just made sure I was okay, then left as firetrucks and police started to swarm the scene. I saw the driver who hit me stopped down the road for a moment, his bumper lying not too far from my feet. He, too, fled as the police arrived. I called my parents to let them know what happened, and they arrived shortly after my call and successfully managed to help me believe the accident was my fault. It was my fault for being out so late. My choices had brought trouble into my life once again. I spent the rest of that weekend in despondent introspection, pondering the purpose of my life.

Travel started to pick up again like a dazzling distraction. I took the chakra practice with me, leaving Lee and everything else I didn't want to confront in my life behind. I downloaded chakra meditations on my phone and listened on the plane as well as in the mornings before the day started. I was back and forth to Europe a few times before extending my stay for a brief residence. I spent three months living in a quaint town in Switzerland, traveling between Paris and Lyon for work, though it seemed too enjoyable to consider it work. I was the only nonmedical professional in a group of world-renowned surgeons, standing in the Institut du Cerveau in Paris, learning about the history of surgical treatments. It was an amazing honor to witness those humans so hungry to help other humans struggling with unpredictable disease progression in the body. My hands were turning pages in books hundreds of years old, the same pages generations prior had used to record their thoughts on the matter. I continued learning through observation, spending every day thereafter in the operating room with those same surgeons. It was a teaching hospital yet still difficult at times to follow what they were doing, as many did not speak English. One surgeon from Peru spoke English and was kind enough to translate for me when we broke bread between cases. We broke bread, literally. The small cafe in the hospital offered soup and baskets with loaves of bread on each table. It was special, simple, and satisfying. There was another side to those amazing experiences though, which nobody saw in social media pictures.

I was alone, in a foreign place, where people didn't look like me or speak like me. I still remember the first day I had off there. I woke up and cried as I struggled with the desire to crawl into the fetal position and stay in bed, afraid to face an unknown place by myself. Due to the time zone difference, nobody at home was awake, so I couldn't call anyone for support either. It was a well-designed day. I was forced to face a fear, without input from anyone else. After a few minutes of considering what I was afraid of, I concluded that I didn't *have* to engage with anyone. I could venture on my own and take the rest as it came. I started the day with a cup of coffee, which was the most interaction I planned for. I smiled at the barista and muttered, "Caffe." It wasn't so bad; I survived. The weather felt more like spring than it did winter, so I didn't necessarily need transportation. I could rely on my own two feet to get me around, which I had never felt more grateful for. So that's what I did—I walked for eight straight hours around Lyon—through two thousand years of history. I passed through breathtaking valleys and beautiful neighborhoods. I sat on street-side benches watching people go about their daily routines, observing how they interacted with one another, how they ate together. My heart couldn't help but smile when I passed by schoolyards, hearing laughter from the voices of little ones. On one passing, a ball popped over the fence and rolled along the path I was walking. The little boy who lost it braced the metal fence rungs, hollering, "Madam! Madam!" at me for assistance. Don't ask me why, but that was the highlight of my day. I was cherishing humans and life in the simplest ways I never knew I could.

Something changed me on that trip, and to this day, the only way I can describe the feeling is *soft*. My heart felt softer when I arrived home. Not many people at the office back in the States found value in the experiences I'd had while overseas. I started to care less about the quality of my work and ended up caving in to spending more time with Lee. I did not want to lose her, and the option to keep her as only a friend was diminishing by the day. She eventually found a job and submitted her resignation, leaving no more excuses for me to leverage in my caustic lack of humility. She asked me out to dinner the night of her last day, to which I of course agreed to in celebration of her new position. I was proud of her for making the move, for getting more money and professional acknowledgment, both of which were long overdue. I talked to her a lot about that as we ate. She finally interrupted my distracting dialogue by standing up to lean across the table to kiss me. I laughed uncontrollably, which immediately made her visibly uncomfortable. I apologized profusely, going on further to say I loved her as my best friend. I started drinking heavily; it was the only way I could imagine facing the rest of the night. She came home with me after dinner. No need to go into further detail than that.

People asked if we were a couple, since we went everywhere and did everything together for a few months after that. I never gave a clear answer, nor did I feel compelled to identify as gay. She was my friend. I loved her dearly in that respect, and that was that. It didn't feel like anything more or anything less. I was willing to make a moral compromise for myself in order to avoid hurting her. That felt like the right thing to do, in the name of love. That was the kinder side of my heart's thinking. I'd be misleading if I didn't say there was something else about it too.

A couple of months before all of this started, you had kissed me. Which left us in a very awkward position, since I didn't know how to respond and did not feel anything from it. Once you knew I was talking to Lee and refused to believe it was platonic, and whether you intentionally meant to or not, you made me feel like I was the most unattractive and undesirable person on earth. You also made me feel like I was incapable of pleasing another. So, when things happened with Lee, and they happened for hours at a time at an electrifying pace,

I thrived off of that as proof that I was not unattractive or undesirable. That I could prove you wrong for how pathetic you made me feel.

We slept at her place more than I would have liked, since she lived with her parents. It was incredibly awkward, emerging from her bedroom together to see her parents at breakfast. The elephant in the room was so large it seemed to consume all available oxygen. It was never discussed, why I was otherwise comfortable sleeping in the same bed with her if we were just friends. Her mother was kind and made a genuine effort to get to know me. She invited me to cook with her and even taught me some of her favorite recipes. While we sat and waited for the food to finish, she told me stories about Lee as a child and showed me pictures of her as a little girl. I remember looking at those pictures and feeling a strong sense of conflicting emotions. It was so wonderful for someone to be willing to connect with me on such an emotionally intimate level, yet at the same time I had to swallow the reality of the situation—which was looking at her as a child and knowing the illicit acts we had committed. I did my best to keep my composure and speak in ways that reassured this mother that I was not there to intentionally hurt her daughter. The truth of the matter was I knew pain was imminent. Those interactions, while sweet and sincere as they were, made the relationship all too real. I didn't want that. And I knew that no matter how much I was willing to momentarily compromise, I could not do it permanently. I found myself in an unusual position of regret. Lee was someone's daughter. She was once a precious baby to her mother and father, a little girl greatly cherished and loved. She was a human, not a possession to be consumed or an accessory to deception. I left that day feeling a deep and true love for her, as well as utterly confused as I wholeheartedly did not know how to express it in any other way than intimacy. That made everything even more confusing, because expressing love in an intimate way was not at all the translation of love welling from within me.

The recreational drug use and promiscuity came to an unexpected halt around December of that year. A noticeable weight started to fall over my soul after Thanksgiving, as if an end of sorts was near. I was never a fan of New Year's—always hated it, actually. If I had a choice of how to spend it, I would watch the ball drop and go to bed. Yet, every year, there was some sort of party to either host or attend. That year, there were a few parties I was invited to across the city. Something in my gut told me to just stay home though. It would be the first New Year's my parents did not host a party either. Every year prior, they had an open-door policy where neighbors and friends would pop in and out all night, playing games, eating tons of food, and drinking heavily into the early-morning hours. That year was quiet, a bit somber even. My mom-mom was not feeling well. She had been in and out of the hospital with heart complications and was generally in a weaker health state compared to previous health challenges. I spent that entire New Year's Eve lying on the couch next to her, memorizing her hands, the way they looked and the way they felt when she lovingly rubbed my back. Something told me that time was running out with her, and that changed everything for me.

With peace and gratitude,
Chole

Mortality

Dear Addie, may this note find you well.

The year to come would later be known as the year of death in my family. Leading up to that point, I was staying at my home up north more on weekends. My mom-mom would still call to either ask me to come over or go pick up something for her from the store. The rest of my family lived closer, so on many occasions, I ignored the calls, hoping someone else would help. The guilt of those decisions still permeates my heart sometimes to this day, like a thorn that serves as a reminder when needed. I didn't feel guilty for not doing what she asked—I knew she didn't really want anything from the store—I felt guilty because she just wanted company. I knew that and blatantly disregarded her need for physical presence as a lonely, sick widow. I wasn't doing anything noble, or even productive, for that matter. I was entertaining a source of pleasure and acceptance for myself. Entertaining selfish desires while she sat in her home alone. My mother, of course, took care of her, cooking her meals and stopping over a few times a day. She was working at the time, though, and unable to stay more than a few minutes each time she was there. Mom-mom didn't want food or paper towels; she wanted companionship. I had the opportunity to comfort another human in their time of need, like she had for me for so many years before that, and I disregarded it because there was nothing in it for me. That revelation came to the forefront of my mind when I answered her call around lunchtime that late Saturday morning.

She said she wasn't feeling well and wanted me to take her to the hospital. Previously, it would take a song and dance, and a fight, to get her to see a doctor when she was sick. The fact that she was asking to go was frightening. In denial, I asked her what was so wrong and why my mom couldn't take her or one of my siblings, since they lived closer. She replied with six words in a stern, authoritative manner: "I need you to take me." My whole body felt like someone had injected me with anesthesia as I hung up the phone. I couldn't feel anything; my mind felt completely numb, following suit of my limbs. I paused for a moment before quickly packing an overnight bag to try to process the fact that I might have just had the last phone exchange with her for the rest of my life. I went into my closet and threw whatever was in reaching distance into a bag, left Lee there, and raced to my car. I sped well over the speed limit for most of the way.

When I arrived, I found her sitting upright on the couch. She was calm and very weak. My heart was racing so heavily I could feel the beats protruding through my chest skin. I felt helpless in the most powerless of ways. I asked if she could walk with me to the car or if she wanted me to call an ambulance. She couldn't walk and did not want an ambulance, so I picked her up and carried her in my arms as if she were child-size. The ride was quiet as I held her hand. I don't think we had ever driven in silence before, except for maybe one time before that. I was frustrated that chores were taking so long one day. We were sitting at a red light on our way to another store, and the light seemed to have been broken; it was taking so long to change. I was tapping my fingers incessantly on the console in an immature display of impatience. She grabbed my hand and squeezed it until I stopped. I gave a smirk and calmed down. Now, her hand wasn't that strong anymore. She was slipping away from me, and there was absolutely nothing I could do about it.

As we worked our way through triage, I continued trying to get in touch with other family members. My mother and sister were at a bridal shower and not answering their phones. My aunt lived farther away and was at least another hour out, while my uncle was at work, not answering his phone either. I held her hand the entire time as they removed her clothes in exchange for a gown and what seemed like a thousand wires connected to her tiny chest. As we were wheeling down the hall to the ICU, she asked me if we were home yet. I told her that we had just driven to the hospital and that we were not home. She asked me a second time, to which I replied again with a more somber tone, "No, Mom-mom. We are at the hospital." After another minute, she squeezed my hand tightly and asked again, "Am I almost home?" That third time clicked. She wasn't asking if she was almost home to where she lived; she wanted to know if she was almost home in heaven with Jesus. My eyes welled up as I squeezed her hand in return and told her, "Yes, Mom-mom, you are almost home." Those were the last coherent words she spoke.

Family started to arrive, devastated by the scene in addition to the fact that Mom-mom was no longer cognizant when they arrived. I've never seen my mother so distraught. I saw her face for the first time as a child, not crying, just staring like a small, scared child at the sight of her dying mother, who she adored and loved so deeply. The doctor pulled us aside and said she was in congestive heart failure, and they were not sure yet if there was anything they would be able to do to reverse it. The next twenty-four hours would be critical in which turn she would take. Two years before this, we had lost my great-aunt, my mom-mom's sister Cassie. It brought me back to that time for a moment …

Her son had been by her side in the hospital, but he did not stay overnight in an effort to get more solid rest. I asked if I could sleep in the chair next to my great-aunt's bed because something told me she should not be alone that particular night. By that point, she was no longer coherent either. I remember texting you, seeking comfort and compassion. You replied asking if it was the wrong time to tell me that you were attracted to me. I could have thrown up. I was sitting next to a dying woman, and that was your reply. I kept staring at the words you sent, so focused on your selfish desires. I wasn't as offended as I was convicted, since my heart was unable to refrain from the glimpse in the mirror of my own disrespect for life's value. I stopped responding and put my phone away. In the middle of the night, Cassie started to try to sit up, reaching her hands strongly in the air. Startled, I asked her what she wanted and if she was okay. She neither looked my way nor acknowledged my questions. She did it three more times that night, each time speaking a very clear and firm request of "Hurry up!" Someone else was in the room with us, someone she clearly felt comfortable speaking to like that, in a place she clearly wanted to go. She died the following day.

Mom-mom had now made the same gesture and spoken the same message twice. Nobody knew what she was doing, but I did. The words she spoke after that did not make sense to most of us. She was looking at everyone around the bed, my mom and her siblings and us, calling her children names of people who had already passed away. Twenty-four hours passed, and instead of discussing options for treatment, we were walked through the process of death. We learned that Mom-mom had already experienced the initial stages weeks before when she stopped eating, as if her body had instinctively known it did not need fuel anymore. Her energy had also drastically declined, ushering the onset of severe fatigue. Now, it was a matter of breathing and bodily shutdown, with the seconds between breaths signaling the proximity of death. They moved her to a private room with a secluded common area for us to eat and sleep if needed. I sat on her right side for the next twenty-four hours, watching her chest rise and fall and counting the seconds between each breath. I didn't eat or sleep. The only time I left her side was to use the restroom.

After forty-eight hours, the nurse told us we should go home to shower and refresh, that none of us knew how long this would go on. Nobody wanted to leave, but the nurse was right. This could go on for days, maybe even weeks. Only God knew how much time Mom-mom had left on earth. I left with my mother for a short, fifteen-minute drive home. We walked in the front door to the phone ringing. It was the hospice unit; Mom-mom died a few minutes after we left. My mother was devastated. All I could think was that Mom-mom knew how hurt everyone was already. Maybe she wanted to spare us the pain the final moment would have permanently ensured, so she endured until we left.

I walked through the next few days beside my mother in a sense of heartbreak that felt inhumane. We shopped for clothes to bury her mother in, as well as made the burial arrangements. Since Mom-mom lived in an apartment, we had little time to clean out her place, so we also had to dispense of the remains of her earthly belongings prior to the funeral. I just wanted life to stop for a minute or at least pause long enough so we could process the colossal voids in our hearts. My mother and her siblings asked me to give the eulogy. I accepted the honor, unsure as to whether I'd be able to say anything without weeping. Mom-mom was my best friend, the only human being on earth I felt understood by. The only human on earth I could run to when I was scared or upset. The only human on earth who welcomed me without question when I showed up unannounced. I didn't trust anyone else. I didn't feel truly emotionally safe with anyone except her. It was as if my only source of unconditional love had been hastily expunged from my life.

I made it through the eulogy without making a mumbling fool of myself. So many things I would have said differently if spoken today. It's not realistic to prepare words to describe the lifetime of one you love in the same season you lost them. Nature of the bereavement beast, I suppose. My parents hosted a beautiful luncheon after the funeral at our local country club. Of course, the open bar was taken full advantage of, by me as well. We were off again at that point, yet for some reason, all I wanted was sympathy from you. I wanted to know you had the capacity to care, that you had the capacity to consider another beyond yourself. I was receiving messages from everyone else I knew all day, except for you. Without fail, you would say, "I love you; if you ever need anything, I'm here," before pulling away again. Yet you were never anywhere to be found when I needed you. My mother was still in shock, tormented with grief, while my father drank to avoid feelings. I was angry at my father for his selfishness when I, myself, didn't even consider the fact that my mother had just lost her mother. I was too self-absorbed to see that she had nobody to console her. Their house filled up with people after the luncheon, where more drinking ensued. I couldn't take it anymore. I didn't want to think, let alone speak to another person about some random nonsense as if it were just another day. I drank a glass of wine and a double dose of NyQuil so that I would go into a deep enough sleep to be away from the world for a while. I crawled into bed in my childhood room and switched my phone to silent so that I could guarantee zero disturbance.

I need silence and darkness to sleep. I've never been the type to be able to sleep with the TV on or even a nightlight. The NyQuil cocktail started to take effect, and it was the first time I felt any kind of peace and reprieve from anxiety all day. Then started an incessant on-and-off glow from my phone screen on the bedside. I picked it up with blurry eyes to turn the phone over so the screen would be facing down, and in the process, I caught a glimpse of seventeen missed calls. It was Lee and her friends. They left voice mails threatening to graffiti my house with malicious innuendos claiming I was a sexual predator. In my drowsy and depressed state of mind, I could not process what could have possibly aroused such insatiable defamation. I had effectively compromised all of my remaining morals for her. I buried my original best friend on the same day my supposed best friend proved to be a bigger fraud than I was.

I powered off my phone, afraid of what was potentially happening to my home up north but too sedated to do anything about any of it. I missed Mom-mom so much. More so, I missed the source of safety, encouragement, and unconditional love she was for me on earth. In the hopelessness of such needs and wants, I found Mom-mom in my dreams that night. I was in my parents' home looking all over for her and came to find her sitting at the dining room table, in the seat she always sat in. She had a cup of tea in front of her and smiled as she stretched out her hand toward me. She told me to come with her, that it was also my time to go. I stood and stared at her, stunned to see her alive as I contemplated her invitation. She stretched her arm farther and said, "Come, Chole. It's your time too." Part of me wanted to go; however, my feet would not move. She stood up from her chair and said it a third time. After a slight hesitation, I physically felt myself take a step toward her. Just as I was about to take the next step to grab her hand, I woke up gasping for air as if I were surfacing from underwater. I didn't want to wake up. I didn't want to face the fact that Mom-mom was still dead. Nor did I want to deal with the drama ensuing in my personal life. I was alarmed that I wanted to go with her. I had the dream two more times that week, solidifying the fact that it was not a result of the NyQuil cocktail I had the night of the funeral. I didn't tell anyone about the dreams until my mother came to me with one of her own. She essentially described my same dream, except her role was in watching our exchange from afar. She told me not to trust the dreams, as they were just that, dreams. She also said she did not get a good sense from the dream she had and that it scared her for some reason. The third dream had a different element than the first two. In the first two dreams, it was just Mom-mom and I, while in the third, I saw my mother's presence—only her hand, actually, on my right shoulder. When Mom-mom told me to come with her that time, she had a red tint in her eyes. As I took a step toward her to get a closer look, I felt my mother's hand grab the back of my shirt and pull me away. It wasn't my mom-mom in those dreams; it was a wolf in sheep's clothing. Interestingly enough, that's what Lee turned out to be.

Our transient time as a couple came to an abrupt halt. I attempted to face her, to meet her in person to understand what I had done to deserve the character assassination the night of Mom-mom's funeral. I wasn't innocent, but I didn't think I had earned such abominable verbal abuse. I knew she didn't read the Bible because she had admitted so on countless occasions whenever we talked about it. Yet, that day, she knew scripture, specifically how sinful it was to do what we were doing. I was speechless to find out that that was her reasoning, that she was ironically the one to end things when I hadn't wanted to start them in the first place. She was the one who had pursued me. She was the one who had not accepted no for an answer. I asked her how her interpretation of that scripture applied to all the random sex she had with countless random men or how it applied to her obsession with pornography. She held strongly to her convictions that those all involved men and that homosexuality was a greater sin. I was not well versed in scripture at that time, yet even then, that sounded exceptionally absurd—for sins to have a scale to them, as if one is okay and others are not. We sounded more like humans trying to play God than accepting God's ways on the matter. As our senseless arguing continued in front of her parents' house, I started Googling scripture to see if what she was saying was really true. She was convinced that the sin of same-sex interaction truly exceeded that of all other immoral sexual acts, going further to say that sexual interactions with the opposite sex really had no limits, as that was more aligned with God's intentions for the relationship. Seeing as I was not going to change her mind, I took a deep breath and ceased all rebuttal. I told her that despite what she thought of me, I still thought she was a beautiful human being and that I loved her regardless. As I turned to walk away, she shouted, "Stop trying to be so perfect! You're not Jesus Christ!" To which I replied, "I know I'm not, but I want to be!" I meant everything I said, and truly felt a sense of unconditional love for her. Even still, there was a brewing notion of conviction. It didn't feel like guilt, yet it didn't feel good either.

Dumbfounded, angry, and embarrassed, I drove home sobbing in utter disbelief at how she could have been such a betraying hypocrite. Not to mention how unrepentant she was of what she and her friends did to me the night of my mom-mom's funeral. No apology, no remorse. No acknowledgment of how she had initiated the relationship or accountability for her intense advances. I felt like an absolute fool, like a complete sellout for how she had used God—the one thing she knew meant the most to me—against me. I got back to my house and sat on the floor against the wall in the living room and cried for hours. I wasn't upset because of what she did or the fact that we were over. I was upset because I had believed I had a real friend. I'd believed I had found someone I could trust with my brokenness. I felt more used than ever before. I never told her I abhorred the thought of being in an intimate relationship with her or that I had had to be drunk and high to engage in it. I wanted her to feel love, even if it meant sacrificing my beliefs in the process. I thought my choice to compromise myself was an act of love. I wasn't confident that true love would leave me feeling exposed, condemned, and ashamed. My search for truth on the matter was still in its infancy.

By that point, it was early spring. I was traveling and rebounding once again with work. I started spending more time with my grandmom as well, my father's mother. Her health was unexpectedly declining at the same time her heart began opening to the idea of receiving help. We would run errands to the food store or bank, then go out to dinner. I would stay overnight and head back north to work the day after. We kept that routine for about five months, until the stress of the holidays drove me back into hiding. The holidays always had a way of promising happiness yet delivering only discouragement. The weight of unrealistic expectations was still alive and well with people asking who I was dating or why I wasn't married yet. All I wanted was for any one person to understand that those things were not who I was. I didn't care if everyone agreed; I wanted just one person to love me for me.

A few weeks before Thanksgiving, my grandmom and I were out to dinner, and this topic came up. The moment she asked who I was dating, I deflected by asking what she was going to order. That generated a moment of silence as we both held our menus in front of our faces like walls. After a minute, she lowered hers and said, "You ought to be nicer to your father." I lowered mine and said, "You first." Stunned by my reply, she asked what I could possibly mean by that. I told her that my father had never felt loved by her, that she never told him she loved him nor treated him like she did. She never encouraged him or acknowledged anything he achieved. She was hypercritical of his life; nothing he achieved was ever good enough for her to approve. I think that's why he drank, but I never said that much. I did tell her that's why I was so mean to her when I was young though. I couldn't stand the way she treated him; it broke my heart. We went on to have one of the most open and authentic conversations of our lives together. It was sad in a way, though, that it had taken so long to be vulnerable and honest. Before we went to bed that night, she called me her angel and her friend. She shared a lot about herself that I know had to be difficult to say. I didn't pay her the same respect; I listened but was not as forthcoming.

Thanksgiving came, and the tradition of everyone traveling in to stay at her house had started. I couldn't handle it. My parents were calling and telling me not to tell anyone about who I dated because they were still mourning my mom-mom and couldn't handle the embarrassment. I started having panic attacks just thinking about spending the long weekend with people who considered me to be an embarrassment and a disappointment, especially those who at the same time swore they loved me. Even after moving away, I had never missed a birthday or holiday with my family. This year was going to be different. I had to resist tradition and reverence for family gathering in an effort to make a stand for myself. Full-court press started with aunts and uncles calling to see if they could change my mind about coming. Everyone thought I was seeking acceptance for my sexuality, when that really had nothing to do with it. They were so far from understanding who I really was or why I did the things I did. I was lost and approaching a very dark place in my life, but they couldn't see that. I had been dating a woman for a few weeks at that point. She was recently divorced and the daughter of a highly publicized executive in the financial district—the perfect accomplice to my cause, at what seemed to be the utmost opportune time in my life. The home she grew up in was a four-million-dollar estate, and she had full access to her family's vacation homes. I transitioned from one fantasy life to the next, diminishing the value of responsibility through unmitigated rebellion.

I remember when you reached out to me; it was right before Thanksgiving, just like clockwork. The holidays were approaching again, so I expected to hear from you. I responded to your questions that indirectly sought to know if I was in a relationship or not. Even though Lee was no longer in the picture, I lied and told you that I was happily in a relationship with her, in hopes of leaving you jealous and as lonely as you always left me. If only you knew the truth.

Thanksgiving was a big event in my family. Each day of the long weekend had an associated tradition. On Wednesday night, the night before Thanksgiving, everyone would gather at my grandparents' house to prepare the food for the following day. The kitchen was crowded with stories from the time since the last gathering as everyone sipped wine and worked together to chop vegetables and prepare fixings for the feast. Thursday was Thanksgiving dinner, and Friday was a hike in the woods followed by pasta dinner. That string of events happened every year without fail. There I was, trading decades of tradition for time with a total stranger, ever so desperate to prove my point—which was that love was far more vast than the closed-minded version I failed to live up to. I called my grandparents' house Thanksgiving night to speak with my grandmom. I wanted to tell her the truth about why I wasn't there. I was shaking. I was so terrified at the thought of her reaction. We had just gotten so close, and now I was going to ruin it by telling her about my corrupt, immoral behavior. Being the strict Roman Catholic she was, I knew there was no way she would ever think the same of me. I cared more about telling her the truth at that point than I did accepting her likeness for a lie, so I started to tell her how hurt I was that nobody could accept me for me and how I had done a lot of bad things rebelling against all of that. Before I could go any further, she interrupted me, saying she had something more important to tell me. She said she needed me to know that she loved me, that she was so proud of me for how hard I worked and how much I had accomplished on my own. She told me that I was forever her angel and that she could not thank me enough for the joyous friendship I had brought her over the previous months we'd spent together. I told her I loved her and let her get back to the gathering there. I hung up and collapsed to my knees in agonizing tears.

Her grace struck my heart. She caught a glimpse of the real me, even if it was just for a minute. And I caught a glimpse of the real her. The strict, materialistic, self-righteous Catholic person I had protested against my entire life was, like me, a facade—a series of arrogant masks adorned to protect an otherwise fragile and vulnerable heart. Her softened heart convicted mine of stone, to the point where I didn't understand who I was or what I was doing anymore. Two days later, I received a call from my mother that Grandmom was in the hospital after her breathing drastically declined. Knowing there weren't many folks who would want to be around me after the stunt I had pulled for

Thanksgiving, I didn't rush down. I had to make sure I was dressed in a very expensive outfit, with perfect makeup and hair, looking well and sophisticatedly content. I couldn't possibly let them see me in the truly disturbed state my soul was in. I arrived the following day to find Grandmom had already been moved to hospice. Once again, death swept in like a thief in the night. I walked into her room to find her in a coma-type sleep. My aunts and my father were in the room with her, looking like little children as they wept with deep grief at the sight of their dying mother. The last conversation I'd had with her was the last conversation I would have. I hugged her and whispered in her ear that I loved her. As I pulled away, I saw her mouth form into a smile. Something in that made me know she heard me and that, even more so, perhaps she forgave me for not being there for her last Thanksgiving. I wasn't so forgiving of myself.

Relentless in my pursuit to prove I was happy with my life, I didn't stay at my parents' home for the funeral. I booked a night at a fancy hotel in the city and attended all of the services as if I was delightfully dating this woman, divorced from my family. I also boycotted the remainder of the holidays, another first in my life. I chose instead to spend the most wonderful time of the year in desperate loneliness with a stranger, in places where people seemed to believe money could buy happiness. I always enjoyed Christmas in New York, to a degree. Handel's *Messiah* paired with a bold culinary adventure, and maybe a stroll past Rockefeller Center with a snack of warm chestnuts was enjoyable enough for me. That year, however, turned Christmas from magical to material. We shopped in stores with prices on sweaters equal to that of my car payment. Yet, in this season, no amount of money was too much, and no amount of extravagance was enough. As if buying things could fill the void in my heart that reconciliation with my family should have occupied. I remember going back home a couple of days after Christmas to exchange gifts with my family, ensuring I looked my best in one of the lavish outfits I had just acquired. I figured if I looked like I was happy with money and meaningless relationships, they would have no reason to disapprove. The price tags of their gifts to me were nowhere near what I had experienced the week prior, yet they meant more to me than anything in the world. I couldn't let them see that though because then they would have proven once again that they were right. I was fine being silently miserable if it meant they were still wrong about me.

My sole source of remission remained to be alcohol, which I was starting to need on a daily basis in order to keep the lies believable. New Year's had come again, and I just could not bear to be at my parents'. Too many memories of Mom-mom and too much fresh pain from Grandmom. I wanted to be far, far away from that scene. I did consider a compromise, especially since my father was not handling the loss of his mother well. I was angry with him a lot, yet I never stopped caring about his well-being. He was starting to have issues at work, falling asleep on the job, along with other signs of depression. I had never known him to let anything interfere with his work, so something was clearly wrong. I spent the remainder of December steady in stubbornness at a ski resort, sipping champagne at night and pretending to be a snow bunny during the day. January's raw and dreary weather was complementary to my bitter and callous heart. I had plans to go home the weekend after New Year's to see my family; however, that came and went, as I still couldn't face them.

The whirlwind relationship I was in ended faster than it had begun, causing me to spiral in madness as each plan I devised for my life backfired on me. It was near the end of the month, shortly after the one-year anniversary of Mom-mom's death. My mind started to betray me as I romanticized thoughts of disappearing. Nothing good was happening in my life, no matter how hard I tried to make it appear so. I made it back home to be with my mom for the anniversary of Mom-mom's death. My father was instructed by his doctor at work to get some medical tests as a precaution, given his lethargy at work and the danger it presented working in an oil refinery. The tests showed that he was severely low on red blood cells and was in critical need for a blood transfusion. The local community hospital diagnosed him with anemia; however, at the same time, they admitted that they did not have the advancements to understand if there was anything more serious underlying. After speaking with doctors at some of the country's most renowned cancer centers for second and third opinions, a unanimous diagnosis was discovered. Just two months after his mother died, my father was diagnosed with a deadly form of bone marrow cancer. He wasn't anemic. His body was no longer producing red blood cells. In the span of eleven months, I witnessed my parents lose their mothers. I lost my source of acceptance, my source of reconciliation, and now was facing the loss of my father, who was the root of everything else. I couldn't imagine him dying without some level of rapprochement and forgiveness. I loved him more than words in existence could describe, and in the grandest acts of selfish pride, I spent my days rebelling a cause that held zero meaning in the face of death.

I had an epiphany moment, you could say, spurred from one too many endings that year. What was the purpose of humanity, if each human's goal was to live and obtain for themselves? If each person's purpose is to achieve their own sense of happiness, comfort, justice, and love? Was I the only one that saw the destructive flaws in a self-governed mindset? Furthermore, how colossal was the limit I myself set on love by imprisoning it with such self-centeredness? I was wasting time, as if a tomorrow was perpetually guaranteed. I was behaving as if there was no end, no purpose other than gratifying my own desires, treating time as if it were obedient to *my* will. The element of self-control, the fruit of the Spirit defined on that little note on the corkboard in my childhood bedroom, was obviously and completely absent from my life. Just because I believed my emotions were the correct bases for my decisions didn't make that right, any more than did believing I could love independently from God make it truth. My choice to serve a selfish conquest rendered self-control, along with all the other fruits of the Spirit, null and void. It was becoming evident that all that mattered at the end was how well we loved, God and one another, sacrificially. I also realized in that moment that I didn't really know the God that I was pledging dis-allegiance to.

With peace and gratitude,
Chole

Damaged

Dear Addie, may this note find you well.

Do you remember the card you gave me the third Christmas after we met? Leading up to that gift exchange, I remember feeling vast emotions of confusion and anticipation. The confusion derived from a place of deep, authentic love for you, which saddened me that it never seemed to align with the love you had in mind. I kept anticipating it though. When I responded to you after each time you had ceased communication without reason or notice, I expected you to realize grace. When I befriended you without judgment as you walked in and out of my life, I expected you to know mercy. When I was by your side when others had abandoned you, I expected you to understand unconditional love. In your card that year, I anticipated an account of your recognition of those things. While your words portrayed a buried interest in such unrestrained love, you concluded with uncertainty as to how it, or I, fit into your life. I'll tell you now what my physical response then displayed. I received that card, and the ones thereafter just like it, with sadness and disappointment. These mixed emotions instilled doubt in the love I had for you and, even more, disappointment for the way I was living it. If I was loving you according to the true definition of love, would confusion and defiance still ensue? Not according to what I was starting to learn from Jesus. There is no confusion or fear in love, for true love drives out those things. As time went on, I started to realize that perhaps the love I was seeking to urgently reconcile had met its opposition in the face of the cultural draws threatening to mislead me. Nevertheless, I still had an undeniable commission on my heart regarding you that surpassed emotion and reason, as you well know.

By this point, we were off again, having exchanged an email or two, just enough communication to maintain a connection of sorts. At the very least, we confirmed each other still existed, maybe even still cared. Of course, I made my life out to be going better than well so that you could feel like a fool for not befriending someone like me. All, of course, to also hide the fact that an internal storm was brewing bigger and badder than I had ever encountered before. I was still wresting with thoughts of existence, struggling to understand who I was and what the purpose for continuing to live was. There was still no safe space to concede, and let's face it, nobody wants to get near a mess like that. Those are the types of thoughts you share that nobody knows what to do with. It's the kind of outreach you seek a pastor or priest for that warrants a response of "I'll pray for you" as the person walks away, as if you just told them you had leprosy. I wouldn't have let anyone near my darkness if they tried anyway. That's what bothered me so much about all the people who continued to say they loved me back then. They knew the wild version of Chole that lived to have fun and party. The Chole on social media who was thriving in a lucrative career, traveling the world on one adventure after another, succeeding and living a vibrant, fulfilling life. Nobody is going to post a selfie of themselves crying on the floor, pictures of the shameful acts they commit in the middle of the night, images of the hurt they cause others, or posts that admit the lies they tell to keep themselves from looking like a terrible person. Nobody knew the wickedness that was inside of me, and I could not trust anyone to stick around after they saw just how broken, hopeless, and unhappy I really was. Without knowing this darker side of me, without knowing my full story, I knew people didn't actually love me for me. They loved an idea of me. That was precisely the hustle I played. In exchange for acceptance, I would figure out who someone wanted me to be, and I would become that person. I suppose that's why you and I never managed to connect on a meaningful level. And why I could never answer you when you said you didn't know where you ended and I began. I wore the clothes you told me to wear. I ate at the restaurants you wanted to eat at. I liked the same music you liked to listen to. I built walls so high to protect my image that I eventually sealed anything purely special about me inside, along with all of the damaged goods.

The only time I dared to show any kind of vulnerability was in my search for God. I asked a lot of questions to a lot of people, many even strangers. I would be at clubs, sitting at the bar, people watching and asking those around me what they thought God thought of the scene. Everyone misinterpreted my search for God as a search for myself, as some kind of coming-of-age journey that would eventually lead to personal maturity and contentment. I didn't want to find myself, though, and for the life of me, I could not find one person to understand that. I knew who I was, and I didn't like me. I wanted to know God in order to know how he could possibly love me after all of the crimes I had committed against humanity.

In my search, I also started asking people what they thought of me. People seemed to fall in love with me quickly, which was useful in getting them close yet petrifying when it crossed a line into emotions and true feelings that I needed to escape from. It was as if I needed to know what they loved so that I could deduce the depth of my own deception. I decided to have drinks with a fresh ex one night in an effort to gain some immediate perspective. I went into the conversation hoping that exposing the truth about my actions and being vulnerable would lead to some kind of lamentation and acceptance for who I really was. The ex thought it was an invitation for a one-night stand and checked out for most of the dialogue once it was clear my intentions were a bit more purified. I left feeling thoroughly defeated. It wasn't that one exchange that threw me over the edge; it was the manifestation of years of those moments finally revealing themselves to me with new eyes. Everything was either about sex, money, or some self-pleasing power play. I opened myself up in a susceptible and defenseless manner, expecting compassion and forgiveness. Instead, I was mindlessly crushed. I didn't want that life anymore—it was like a chaotic circus ride that I desperately wanted to get off. I didn't want to be in a relationship with anyone. I didn't want sex to be the object of a power exchange. I didn't want to be content with the life I had because it was incredibly superficial and irreverent. I didn't want a career title as my identity, nor the number of zeros in a paycheck that required my soul in exchange. Most of all, I didn't want to lie anymore. I got in my car and started screaming, incomprehensibly disgusted with the skin I was in. I took the back roads home because I felt like I was moving in slow motion, unfit for the highway. Despair and hopelessness were the authoritative figures riding along with me, empowering a desire to not live anymore if this was to be the purpose of my life. In a frenzy, I called my brother. He was a blameless guy, never in trouble as a kid and was growing to be an equally prudent adult. I trusted him because he had a close relationship with the Lord. I called him and told him I didn't want to live anymore. I told him I was in the car and was contemplating the idea of racing into a tree. I had no intentions of actually harming myself; I was, however, infatuated with the idea of dying to everything that was influencing my spiritual demise and self-destruction. Plainly said, I didn't want to live the life I had chosen for myself. I wanted to kill it. He was upset, begging me to pull over and reason with a more permanent solution to these temporary emotions.

I promised him that I wouldn't hurt myself and that I would just go home and go to bed. And that's exactly what I did. I walked in, draped my blazer over the dining room chair, and crawled under the covers. I wasn't in bed for more than ten minutes when my doorbell rang. I couldn't imagine who it could possibly be at that hour and was far too despondent to entertain a surprise guest. I didn't answer it at first, hoping it was someone with the wrong address. Then came a loud, intense bang on the door. That terrified me enough to jump up and run to the window to catch a glimpse of who was out there—it was a police officer. I opened the door, dressed in silk short pajamas. The officer asked if I could step out. I did so out of respect while questioning why he was there in the first place. He told me that he had received a call from someone stating that I was a threat to myself and that he could not leave me there alone. I was beside myself. I pleaded with him to let me stay home, that I was fine and just having a bad night. He said he did not have a choice, given the report, and had an obligation to take me involuntarily. I asked him if I could at least change my clothes, which he also denied, permitting me only to grab the blazer and running sneakers that were within reaching distance. I looked like a fool and felt like a submissive hostage.

There I was, in the back of a police car again, this time completely sober yet somehow equally renounced. I felt too forsaken to even be embarrassed. I had finally reached out for help, this time to someone I truly thought I could trust, and this was what I got in return. When we arrived at the hospital, I was taken to a solitary area and asked to remove all of my clothing in exchange for a hospital robe and slippers. It was the most dehumanizing experience I had ever encountered. I wasn't even offered a glass of water, just left in a room by myself for hours with no contact or communication as to what was going to happen next. There were no windows, not even an aperture on the door. No way of telling what was going on or what time of day it was. All that was in the room was a small cot-like bed with a blanket similar to the steel wool in prison. I lay there staring at the ceiling, mind-numbingly absent of thought. I came to find I was in that state for almost five hours by the time a nurse came in. She unlocked the door with a key and asked if she could enter. I turned my head slowly toward her and said, "Sure," as I dispiritedly moved to sit up. She proceeded to ask me a series of questions to gain an understanding of what had happened. I asked her what time it was before I replied. I had been lying there all night because her shift did not begin until 9:00 a.m. I turned my head toward the floor, wondering how these people could leave someone they thought was in a suicidal crisis alone until it was an obliged and convenient time for them to respond. She asked me a series of questions to see if I had ever hurt myself in the past or if I presently wanted to. She was emotionless, asking monotone questions, then writing down answers, one after the other. I responded with just enough detail to answer her questions, not offering more or less than what was asked. When she was finished her questioning, she looked at me with a weary expression, as if I was a waste of her time. Confused by her nonverbal speech, I asked her what would be happening to me next. She asked me how I felt and why I thought I was there. I told her that I'd used suicidal language to express a distraught feeling of hopelessness and dissatisfaction with my life. She went on to tell me that according to her assessment, she had gathered that I had just had a bad night. Then she asked me to wait there a little while longer until she could clear me to leave.

I lay back down, anticipating her return to be as far off as the first appearance. The door opened unexpectedly and rather quickly after that, except this time, it wasn't the nurse. It was my brother. He stood in the doorway, eyes filled with tears as he leaped toward me. He held me tighter than he ever had in our lives. I continued to lie there, offering an arm for half a hug back, curious if this was what it took to receive some kind of compassionate consideration in life. He couldn't see how deeply it hurt to be treated like that in another one of my darkest hours of need. On our ride home, I asked him why he would do such a thing and if that was the Christian way to treat a broken mess like me. Throw a police officer my way and a night in solitary confinement. Maybe that would cure me. I was angry in the most paralyzed of ways. When we arrived back at my place, I found his girlfriend in my living room, cozy on my couch in front of the fireplace. In an instant, I knew she had done it. She was studying mental health and had an unexplained hatred for me for how close I was with my brother. When I made eye contact with her, she turned cowardly and put her face in my couch pillow. I walked into my room and locked the door behind me. I stood in a hot shower for over an hour, hoping the water would wash away the feelings of shame and betrayal. I was so deeply disturbed by the fact that there was nobody in this world that I could trust to be broken around—that is, without receiving some kind of emotional disservice in return.

I had been considerably against therapy my whole life, until I realized the only basis for my reasoning was because my family held that stance. Therapy was for weak people—furthermore, those mentally *disturbed* people—nevertheless, a demonstration of character weakness in the most public of humiliating ways. That wisdom wasn't plausible enough, given our depth of dysfunction, to rely on anymore, especially given the fact that I was aware of my mental state, and it was indeed disturbing. I was ready and willing to admit that. So, I made the decision to start seeing a counselor. I was twenty-seven years old and living a successful life, for all intents and purposes, seeking to understand why I was so hopeless and resentful. I had more money than I needed, stable work in a lucrative industry, good health and reliable health insurance, a nice home in a safe neighborhood, family that loved me, friends who enjoyed my company, and no rational reason to be stressed. That's what I convinced myself of, at least. I felt guilty for claiming that any part of those things was broken, especially when it came to my family. The weight of the guilt that overwhelmed me at the thought of acknowledging our relational defects was enough to silence me all those years. What I needed was an unbiased, unaffiliated person to share my pain with, to see if it was real. To see if I was irrational for feeling forlorn and aggrieved for my life's journey and subsequent choices.

After a few sessions, my counselor invited me to try a visualization therapy. She suggested that it could help in the process of forgiving, replacing painful memories with positive ones. During the first exercise, she asked me to close my eyes and think back on my childhood to a time when I felt most abandoned and unprotected. My mind instantly went back to that scene in the kitchen I told you about in my first letter. My father was throwing food against the walls, and my mother was on the floor crying and cleaning it up. My brother was a small boy at the time, and that was one of the only times he tried to intervene before me. My father picked him up by the front of his shirt and slammed his tiny body against the refrigerator. Enraged at the sight of that, I entered the scene in an attempt to fight the giant man threatening to bully the physically weaker women and children in his path. He threw me against the windowsill, and I fell to the floor. My back was sorely bruised, along with my defenseless spirit. That was the same night I felt resentful toward God and heard the whispers that initiated my doubt in God's love and care for me. She asked me to stay in that place for a moment. As I did, I saw a movie of sorts, scenes that played in my mind, each one like perfect puzzle pieces coming seamlessly together, connecting the dots between decisions and behaviors that had stemmed from countless nights like that one leading up to where I was at present.

Then she asked me to breathe, to take a few deep breaths and depart from that place. Next, she invited me to think back on my childhood to a time when I felt most whole. I was drawn to memories of my eight-year-old self, the little girl who fearlessly intervened in the faces of school bullies and organized neighborhood wiffle ball games starring the unpopular kids. The little girl with premature empathy from the hurt and suffering she was so intimately witness to. I returned to images of Jesus and the purpose of his life that placed meaning on my heart. The counselor guided me to stand in front of that little girl, to look her in the eyes and recount what she wanted for her life. I gazed into her eyes as if she were standing right in front of me. I wanted to reach out and hug her ... she was so innocent and full of beautiful potential. Before I could embrace her, I collapsed with sorrow. It wasn't until the counselor asked me to open my eyes that I realized my hysterical tears were real. She asked me why I was crying. "I failed her," I said. She reached out with a tissue and asked, "What did you tell her, what did you want for her life?" I wiped my eyes and stood up to leave. "Love," I replied, "I wanted her to be a soldier of love, and I turned her into a citizen of rebellion." The only thing that was undeniable now was my brokenness.

With peace and gratitude,
Chole

Wisdom

Dear Addie, may this note find you well.

I can understand the stigma associated with therapy and counseling, or any suggestion to get help, for that matter. Just the thought of it implies that there is something so inherently wrong that it is impossible to resolve alone, consequently threatening self-defining abilities, value, and worth. Even on a dark, lonely, discouraging path, I viewed the invitation for guidance as an insult to my competence in navigating life as a grown adult—a line of stubborn thought processing that could be traced back to a root that spanned generations preceding my existence. I believed asking for help was a sign of weakness, because that's how the people generations before me viewed it. And yet there I was, comfortably uncomfortable being damaged in front of a total stranger. She asked questions that gently sought to deliver me to a place of understanding, even at the expense of a realization that everything I believed in was born on the basis of other people's opinions and experiences. What may have been more evident was the fact that it was virtually impossible to make sound decisions in the midst of an identity crisis. I was a chameleon of a person, which can be viewed as a good thing in the world, since it essentially means you have the ability to fit in anywhere. The flip side to that is it also meant I did not know what I stood for. There was no basis for my decisions other than my emotions and the emotions of those around me, all of which changed as quickly and as reliably as the tide. My life lacked consistency and stability in more ways than one. I built an identity synonymous with defiance, which welcomed a resentful and angry spirit that existed to express vengeful disapproval of relational vandalism between humans. Hypocritically, I was living out the very thing I had sought to eradicate. At the root of my pompous behavioral reasoning was my father's rigidly unrepentant posture. I blamed his incessant provoking to be the irresistible apple I bit into every time. With hostile intention, I wanted to make him and anyone else who triggered me to feel disrespected, silenced, and undervalued feel the pain I felt. I convinced myself that my actions were of vindictive integrity, in the most lethal of ways.

The more I followed the trails of these branches to their roots in my heart, the more I understood why I did what I did—the exploration phase, if you will, in troubleshooting my current state of demise. The feeling of worthlessness was taking over my soul as I absorbed the criticism on countless occasions about how I wasn't a real woman. When you hear something spoken to you, repeatedly, from authoritative and influential figures in your life, it's hard not to believe it. I lived experiences, between my personal and professional life, which regarded women as the weaker vessel. It made my blood boil beneath my skin as I watched women in my life turn meek and submissive toward men, and furthermore promoted silence in the face of intimidation. The whole competitive dynamic between men and women woke a beast inside of me that persisted in blurring the lines between justice and vengeance.

The question did come up in session: why did I not seek the church or my pastor with these questions since I was perpetually seeking what God thought about it all? Simply said, I did not feel safe. People in the church seemed to adore a narcissist as their leader, which even in my young mind didn't make sense. My pastor growing up was more like a showman than he was an honorable representative of Christ. Behind the scenes in catechism class, if we didn't do as he said, he would assert his authority over us by flipping our desks or throwing paper balls at us. He was emotionally abusive and physically violent when parents were not around, and when they were, his smile returned as if he had a split personality that turned on as easily as it turned off. The undercurrent of church messages on my struggles further solidified the doubts I had in my own value and worth. I wasn't good enough to meet God's standards; that much was clear. What kept me searching was Jesus, a loving male figurehead to a church, defined by a body of people defined by love. Not a building filled with rules, bullying, and oppressive domineering behavior that sought to control people. The language used to describe women and women's role in life between home and the church led me to believe that women were the problem. My father consistently claimed that his drinking was a result of him marrying my mother. Church leaders degraded women as being more vulnerable to temptation since Eve was first tempted and led her husband to do the same. Neither of those depictions aligned with my natural disposition. I was silenced at home, at church, and, later in life, in the workforce for the same reasons. My passion for my work was said to be too aggressive, and my inability to maintain silence in the face of male intimidation was deemed as exaggerated reactions to slight male infractions—most notably caused by me, for being female and sensually desirable. Women were also defined as emotionally charged beings who could not be trusted in leadership roles and needed men to settle them down. This is why I was told on countless occasions to "settle down" and get married. Being a single person in the church was also frowned upon, elevating love in the form of marriage to be the ultimate form, as if those who did not desire to marry were subject to a lonely life absent of love.

So, no, I did not trust the church with my deepest hurts and questions. I didn't have a sense of belonging to believe my greatest vulnerabilities would be handled with care. I broke the feminine ideal. The portrait of a real biblical woman was painted as quiet, meek, submissive, and sweet. And many of the women there fit that mold. They paired conservative sweaters with basic hairstyles. They were reserved, with kind smiles and docile demeanors. I looked and sounded different, wearing blazers with stiletto heels, accompanied by assertive speech and aggressive action. Fear and guilt had already subconsciously consumed me; adding to it was the overwhelming burden of a deeply pervasive culture of religious shame. The gospel, rather "good news," message was a constant reminder to me of how terrible I was, while concurrently holding me in its grasp through fear—fear that I was too wretched to live up to God's standard for a biblical woman, coupled with confusion that rendered a conclusion that God must have made me wrong.

My father's drinking binges were triggered often by being identified as a drunk, particularly when he was called that by a woman—be it his mother, his wife, or me. I could never understand why he would turn into the thing he was being accused of, until I realized I was doing the same thing. Being unable to live up to the expectations your parents have for you is one thing; being told that the failure to live up to those expectations was also against God took my identity crisis to a whole other level. It drove me to a belligerent determination to give people something to really criticize me for. It was the only way I knew to reclaim approval, acceptance, and self-respect. It was an "I'll prove you wrong" kind of reversed immature mentality that did nothing but fail me more than my attempts to change those around me. My father's decisions to choose alcohol and anger as a form of rebellion against his own flawed authoritative figures became my own. His actions and words passed down disapproval, insecurity, and an utter inability to be wrong in the most remorseless of ways. I was now doing the same. He justified his behavior in manipulative ways that in turn made me feel guilty for expressing my discontentment toward emotional abuse. I had developed a keen sense for playing the victim in situations where I was the assailant. I felt a slight repair of the tears in my heart when I realized that I did not hate my father—I loathed myself and my decisions. The surfacing truths that exposed the roots of the *whys* that culminated in who I was were equally as devastating to awaken to. It proved my battle was never against him, or anyone else, for that matter. It was against myself and the spiritual battle within.

The most memorable session I had with my counselor was the night she guided me through an accelerated resolution-therapy exercise. I confessed to her that I had a lot of bitterness and unforgiveness in my heart, so she said this would help by exchanging memories associated with trauma with healthier memories of the person or people associated with the stress-triggering thoughts. Once again, she asked me to close my eyes, this time to picture myself sitting at a campfire. She told me to invite to the fire one person I trusted. I invited Jesus. She told me to invite a second person I trusted. I invited Mom-Mom. With both of them sitting on either side of me, she asked me to invite someone to the fire that I felt anger and resentment toward. I invited my father. The memory I went back to in hopes to exchange was that dreadful night in the kitchen. I chose that night because it yielded the doubt I developed in God's capacity to care for me. She asked me to put myself back there, to pause at the worst moment and look around and take an inventory of the scene. Then she told me to allow the emotions I felt to surface, to feel each one as whole as I could as they came. I felt pain for my mother. Her asthma was so bad she could barely breathe as she worked to clean up the mess. I felt a hopeless kind of sadness for my father, knowing that he must have been hurt in some deep form in his life in order to feel authorized to hurt others, and himself, like he was. I felt a deep ache for our family, for the coexistence of love and hate that diminished love's full potential. The last emotion I felt was disgust, a vengeful bitterness toward the root causes of transgression. I remember taking a few deep breaths in silence before she asked me to leave that scene and go to a time when those same people were together sharing joy.

That one took more time to think about. We had a lot of happy times, just not necessarily complete ones. Joy was always accompanied by arguing or discord at some point or another in the occasion. The place I definitely landed on was my parents' bedroom. On the nights my dad had off from work, he gathered us all into his and my mom's bed to tell us a bedtime story. He would read us a chapter from the Bible, then tell us to close our eyes and imagine we were on a boat. I remember vividly picturing the calm water around us, the sound of night bugs far in the distance, and sharing in the comfort of one another's harmonious closeness. He said to feel the cool breeze and the slow rock of the boat and to feel safe because we were all together. It was like a guided meditation before I ever knew what that was.

I discovered a deep root of love there, deeper than the root of the traumatic memory. I felt safe in the presence of the Word in scripture combined with an unconditional togetherness in that vast ocean. Similarly to before, she asked me to stay in that place and observe everyone in the scene and the emotions that would surface. I felt safe; my dad was a big, strong man with calloused hands from working hard, who I knew would do anything to protect his family. I felt an unexpected sense of compassion for my dad; he had a lot of love to give and had a lot of love in us at his disposal. He just seemed to struggle to receive it, like me. I felt gratitude for the peace we had together, for the calmness for my mom, and for having siblings I not only loved but abided with in friendship. I saw my father through the lens of a child and felt empathy for the hurt he caused from the places of hurt he had collected. I saw a little boy, diminished as a man for not living up to the expectations of his parents. I returned to the campfire with an overwhelming amount of love for my dad as I apologized for all that I had done. I told him I could understand his pain now and that I forgave him too. It all felt so real. I couldn't believe I was sitting in the counselor's office when I opened my eyes.

It was getting noticeably more difficult to work the only ways I knew how. The work I was doing in counseling was softening my heart to a point where I did not want to participate in unethical practices anymore. I didn't want to be affiliated with lies or misleading promises for personal gains. I was starting to feel like I was being used as a pawn in a game bigger than I could even imagine. Of the people traveling to Europe from my company now, I was by far the lowest title holder of all, yet I was expected to do all of the talking and somehow convince key opinion leaders there to remain in union with us. I remember walking into one meeting with just the president of the division with me. He saw the customer we needed to win and told me he was going to hang back because he felt the customer liked me more than he liked him. That was probably the worst move he could have made. We met for a cappuccino, and he didn't sit, so I didn't waste his time with small talk. I asked him to tell me the truth as to why he was so reluctant to work with us anymore. I told him that I genuinely wanted to help and that if he wanted, whatever he shared would not go beyond our conversation. His shoulders relaxed as he began to tell me that the leaders in my division had been lying to him for years. They promised that they would help him expand his product into the United States and never took any real action to do so. He went on to say that every new product-development project he was associated with felt like a joke. Like the division was not interested in real clinical advancement, just in stealing ideas to either acquire or procure cheaper versions of his solutions. He said he didn't trust them anymore, too many years of false promises and lies. He was passionate about what he did and truly loved his patients, and he wanted to work with a company that shared in the same true fervor to help others. He was definitely in the wrong place for that.

This organization had taken advantage of his devotion, a feeling I could presently relate to. It was not a good position to be in for the company, yet I avidly appreciated the honest exchange. It was the first genuine conversation I had ever had in a professional setting, the first humanly authentic dialogue that didn't include some strategic sales tactic or sexual intimidation to swindle the outcome. I took one more sip of my cappuccino and thanked him for his honesty. Then I stood up to leave. He followed, and per etiquette, we exchanged a cheek-to-cheek embrace. I looked him in the eyes and told him the truth, that the company had no plans of ever entertaining his ideas. I told him that I respected his passion and treasured the time he had granted me in his operating room to observe and learn from him. I told him to go, to not renew his contract and take his ideas to a company that would respect them. We embraced again, and I left. When I met up with the president of the division, I told him it was over. He probed for details of the conversation, of which my lips were sealed. Business is business, as most would say. I spent the plane ride home wondering why I ever thought it was okay to deceive, lie, and cheat. I had believed that—that it was all for business and nothing personal. But it *was* personal, because people were always involved. Why was I comfortable with respecting or disrespecting people according to relational circumstances over the fact that we were all equally human?

There was no real reason to go back to Europe after that, so my travel and focus shifted domestically. I had been working closely with a surgeon in the DC area, to develop products to treat more advanced and unpredictable disease states. These were patients who lived every day with uncontrollable and unmanageable symptoms. I observed amputations of fingers, toes, and full limbs. People were losing parts of their bodies to a disease that had prevention potential with the right focus. Before I started working on that project, there was a significant shift in responsibilities at work. There were growing concerns around customer-relation compliance that drove the responsibility to maintain updated consulting contracts to my boss's level. I used to have a contributing role in it, so I knew how much work it took to keep compliant. I didn't trust my boss to carry out those responsibilities well at all; nevertheless, I stepped back and respected the new line that had been drawn. The company made another acquisition, this time in Texas. Since my boss was focusing on ensuring our customers were contractually covered, I was free to fully focus on my actual job of product development. I was in Texas to learn the new portfolio and ensure the existing active projects in the pipeline were complementary. It was as if someone had swooped in and taken all of the work I didn't like, then exchanged it with only the tasks I did. I was enjoying my work more than ever.

There wasn't a slow day to be had. I was juggling five new projects and overseeing the maintenance and obsolescence of sixteen others. One morning while the DC surgeon consultant and I were grabbing coffee before our meeting, he casually mentioned to me that he hadn't been paid for his time on the project for over three months. I, knowing of course who the problem was, promised him I would look into it and apologized profusely for the delay. I followed through first thing the next day and indeed confirmed the root of the problem. Knowing how serious of a compliance infraction this was, I scheduled a meeting with corporate legal counsel to understand what could be done to remediate the situation. I knew it was my boss's responsibility to maintain customer contracts, and I knew he was failing to keep up with his work. Despite my lack of respect for the man and this ripe opportunity to highlight his incompetence, I cared more about resolving the issue for the customer than assigning blame. Legal informed me that his contract had expired four months prior, which meant he had not been under contract the whole time we had been working together. What I was not able to gather was why my boss would have lied to me. I had asked to confirm with him several times over the course of some project milestones, the majority of which I'd communicated in writing so I'd have proof, if this customer's contract was current. Each time, he had affirmed that it was and had even gone further to state that I was approved to continue working with him. I had saved all of the emails where he stated in black and white that he had done so. I didn't think asking my boss for proof of his actions would get me anywhere since he had lied to me on so many previous occasions. So, on my next trip to DC, I asked the customer if he had ever received an updated contract from my boss. He showed me the last communication he'd received from my boss, which was a two-line email telling the consultant that he was working on updating his contract and would send it to him soon. He then proceeded to show me several follow-up emails he had sent to my boss, with no replies. I texted my boss, again in attempt to defuse accusation, asking if there was any way he could have had things confused. I did not neglect to acknowledge the fact that he was the most disorganized manager I had ever had. He held to his original stance, assuring he had done his job. I requested that the customer send one more email follow-up to my boss, this time copying me and our division president on it so that I could escalate the issue with his permission. He wanted to get paid and, like me, despised the consistently deranged results from my boss.

About a week later, I was invited to a meeting with legal, without so much as a purpose or agenda provided. I was served a formal notice of noncompliance with verbal warning that my level of negligence in my work with that customer was under review. Beyond baffled, I reminded the lawyer of my professional role and responsibility in the matter, stating that I had written proof of the negligence from the party truly accountable. I told him that my boss had lied to me and the customer to hide the fact that he had not done his job, and proceeded to show him all of the email exchanges I'd documented. By all facts and accounts, my boss was the person out of compliance—not me. I marched directly back to my desk and proceeded to email the lawyer every piece of communication I had just shown him, including the emails from my boss granting me permission to work with the customer. There was literally nothing to dispute. Later on the same day, I received a meeting invite from the division president. Something bad was happening, and I was starting to get the impression that I was the targeted scapegoat.

I took the meeting with the president, who expressed the purpose of the meeting was to check in on me. He said he'd heard what was going on and wanted to ensure I was okay. His false sense of empathy didn't fool me; his questions were also not authentic enough to prove any real concern for my well-being. He was digging to get a feel for how much proof I had that the negligence lay within his chain of command, because ultimately, it really meant that he was not keeping tabs on his manager's performance. I revealed my hand, telling him everything I had in writing. I was already running late to the airport for another trip to Texas, so I left the conversation there. I was scheduled to be in Texas for a week to aid in merger activities, as well as support a sales training. Two days into the trip, I received another cryptic meeting invite with the division's lawyer; however, this time my boss and another manager were included. The lawyer was in New Jersey, and we were all in Texas, so the meeting was scheduled as a conference call—a rather urgent one, at that.

My boss and his peer pulled me aside fifteen minutes before the meeting, stating that they wanted to align on our story before the meeting. I couldn't help but laugh and ask what story, as I had facts to prove that my boss was responsible for falsely providing me with approval to work in a situation he was accountable for ensuring was sound. Apparently, the customer I was working with had filed a complaint against our company with the governing agency responsible for overseeing compliance. His complaint stated a failure to pay for services rendered, and in addition, it claimed reason to believe a kickback had been offered in exchange for the delay. The exposure had been taken to a much bigger level now, and mind you, this was a time in the industry when there was no place to hide anymore. This company thought they were smaller than the ones I had come from and were therefore exempt from the strict regulations the larger companies had to abide by. That arrogance was proving to turn on them. Legal liability was on the table, and they needed a name to associate charges with. My boss didn't speak a word; he just sat there with a dastardly look on his face, biting his nails like the coward he was.

The other manager did most of the talking, attempting to get me aligned with whatever story they wanted to try to sell. I stood my ground, stating I knew the truth and I had it in writing. I was willing to show it all and confess my involvement on the basis of the instruction I was given. I had nothing to hide—they did. Thirty seconds before the phone rang, he said that the lawyer was going to call and ask for a verbal plea from each of us, since each of us had some kind of relation to the incident. This other manager had the responsibility of being a second set of eyes on all contracts before the president ultimately oversaw the status of each in a monthly update. He suggested that we all plead guilty, so that the blame was dispersed and not piled on any one person. The sheer amount of deplorable timidity pouring out of both of them made my stomach turn. I knew that I had lied and deceived a lot of people in my life, and living through this was showing me firsthand what that looked like from the other side of the table. I was prepared to claim responsibility for my involvement, for perhaps not pressuring my boss enough for proof when there was a clear disconnect between his words and the customer's reality. However, there was no way I was going to be intimidated by these men to take the fall for something I did not do.

The phone rang. Before the other manager answered, he looked at me and said, "Guilty, okay? Here we go." The lawyer read the statements to us and asked how we pleaded in response, requesting that each of us respond as he called our name. He started with my boss's peer, who replied, "Innocent." Next was my boss. "Innocent," again. My body felt like it was on fire, with a ton of rocks being piled on my chest. My name was called last. It took everything in me not to cry and break down in front of them. I looked at both of those men in the eyes and responded, "No contest." I stood up and walked out of the room and down the hall to human resources. I told HR that I was just involved in a considerable case of coercion and that I would be reporting the entire event to the chief human resources officer. The HR representative looked terrified. As I went to leave, I turned around and told her she would also have my resignation in her inbox within twenty-four hours. I called a cab, then from the cab called my airline to get myself on the first flight home. I packed my bag as fast as I could and ran out of my hotel room to the elevator. The elevator doors opened, and there, standing inside, was my boss. I shook my head in disgrace, stunned that he could have the audacity to follow me. He stretched out his hand and said, "No hard feelings?" I looked at him with disgust, signaling him with a head nod to get out of my way. I got on the elevator and made it to the airport in time to make my flight. I could not believe what I had just done. If it isn't clear from how I am communicating it—this was one of the biggest turning points in my life. I finally said no. I finally said enough with exploitation and deceit. For a couple of months leading up to that point, I had been in talks with a recruiter who had a lucrative offer from another company on the table for me, which I had been considering. Now seemed like the opportune time to accept. I emailed her to say as much before the plane took off, then thanked God for yet another way out.

The first thing I did when I arrived back at the office the following day was deliver my resignation to human resources, as I had promised. I was contacted shortly after by the chief officer of human resources, who requested that I come to meet with her immediately. I had never met her before, and given the flurry of legal activity in the past week, I did what she asked. I didn't know what to expect, but what happened wasn't anything in the realm of what I was thinking. She began to plead with me not to leave. She said I was one of the most promising employees they had ever had and that they were ready to create a new position for me in one of their other divisions. She spoke to me as if I was blind to the fact that accolades and a promotion were the consolation prizes for years of sexual intimidation and now a serious false legal accusation. She had the audacity to conclude her pitch by stating, "I will not accept your resignation." I was pretty sure it was illegal to do that. Nevertheless, I told her I would consider her offer. She said she needed a reply by the end of the week, which at that point was only two days away. I submitted for paid time off the following day to meet with the president of the new company I was interviewing with. The salary was 40 percent more than what I was currently making, and the culture was noticeably healthier. In an attempt to shake off the duress from the previous day, I shook his hand and accepted his offer.

When I returned to the office the next day, the president of my division called me into his office for a sit-down. He told me that all of that mess with the consulting contract could be settled with a simple write-up. No legal charges or issuance of noncompliance. That was his take on a generous offer—he wanted me to accept being written up for something I did not do in exchange for his admittance of his managerial oversight. I told him absolutely not, then walked over to the office of the chief officer of human resources to decline her offer as well. I told her how much I truly loved my job and how incredibly sad it was to see the noble kind of work we did be defaced with such blatant corruption. She refused to accept my resignation and insisted that I not deny her offer. I tried explaining how the culture was a severe problem and how changing where I sat was not going to make a difference in that. She went on to offer me a higher title with the new position and more money, to which I further expressed disinterest. I remember her face and her body language so vividly, how noticeably frustrated she grew, with clenched fists, as she realized she could not buy my decision. It felt like I was awakening to a new code of morals and ethics, worth far more than any corporate position or paycheck could match. I told her that the amount of people in high places trying to coerce me was enough evidence for me to believe that the problem was far deeper than what was seen on the surface and that it needed to be eradicated. I respectfully declined her offer for the last time and walked out of her office while she was still speaking her pleas for me to stay. I didn't think to sue or expose them; the truth always has a way of surfacing. That was becoming clear enough in my own life.

I fell ill after that. I had been in and out of the ER for the past two years with symptoms of shortness of breath and pains that would radiate from my midback into my arm and chest. You were there, reluctantly, for one of the earlier instances. I still remember seeing your Roxy slipper shoes beneath the curtain as I was being wheeled back from the CAT scan. Each visit to the hospital resulted in a discharged diagnoses of severe indigestion caused by anxiety. I didn't feel stressed; I felt confused. I felt trapped in a world of extortion, in an identity that caused me to feel captured by the skin I was in. The baths helped me to relax and quiet my mind, even if only for a moment. Yet they were futile in getting me clean.

With peace and gratitude,
Chole

Life or Death

Dear Addie, may this note find you well.

Two weeks into the new job, a former colleague reached out to me. She sent me an email with a link to a news article about the company I had just left. The division I worked for had been raided by the FBI. People were arrested for corrupt sales practices and jailed for billing fraud. Senior leaders were terminated on the spot, and at least one sales manager was sentenced to prison time. I had not trusted my decisions for years, and reading through that made me feel like there was hope. Not necessarily in myself but in the new wisdom I had been gleaning from scripture and the foundation it was saying to form decisions from. There was some evidence that it could be trusted, that prioritizing morals and ethics over money and power had real consequences.

There was a lot of travel involved with the new job too. My first trip was to Nevada, where I had a unique opportunity to immerse myself into learning another area of anatomy and meet new surgeons. I spent a lot of time in the cadaver lab, as it was my first time ever working with the spine. At the end of one of the training sessions, I asked a surgeon if he had ever felt the spinal cord. I told him I was curious what it looked like and what it felt like, given it was the primary agent of bodily function. It took me over an hour to dissect deep enough to make an opening to remove a vertebral body so that I could gain access to the cord. It felt thick and squishy, like a raw clam. My first feeling was awe, awe in God's creation of humans—the intricate detail of every aspect and the undeniable replica between all of us. No matter what pigment the top layer took on, just millimeters beneath the surface, we were all the same. Bleeding the same color blood, living off of the same set of organs, healed with the same medicines, and reconstructed with the same implants. I had worked in thousands of cadaver labs up to that point, none nearly as profound. It could have been the day as well. It was a sunny June day in Nevada, and the only break I took was to make a phone call to my mother, who was at the hospital with my father. As we spoke, my father was receiving a stem cell transplant, the donor being his oldest sister. My mother had convinced me to go on that trip, that there was nothing I could have done other than wait in a waiting room. It was still difficult to be almost three thousand miles from home while that was happening. I was starting to tear up when my boss came running out to tell me I had to get off the phone and come back in. It hurt to have to rush off the phone like that in such a precious moment. Every single moment of my life was prioritized by work and money; I was a slave to them both, no matter how hard I tried to break free.

It was a long day in the lab, followed by a late-night red-eye home. I had to be in the office the next day for meetings, so sleep was also a servant of my schedule. Around midmorning, I started to experience severe upper back pain. It was so uncomfortable I had to ask to leave early. My boss noticed that I was in pain and suggested it may have been from wearing lead for so long the day before. That was certainly a possibility; however, it was worsening to a point where it did not feel muscular.

I had been hanging out with a woman for a few weeks up to that point as well; her name was Edie. We had met online and talked for a few weeks before then. She was the first person I was honest with—as honest as I could be at the time, at least. I told her that I was looking for a friend, someone with shared interests and experiences. When we met, I think we both agreed that we shared some kind of bond, one that was completely based on our level of education, work experience, and tax bracket. She was brilliant and wealthy and shared a similar passion for the medical field. We did the kinds of things that accomplished and cultured people did in New York City, like visit the Met, frequent Broadway shows, spend Saturday mornings sipping coffee from our kayaks on the lake and Sundays hiking the trails along the Hudson River.

Edie had reserved massages for us that night, which we never made it to. I told her I was not feeling well and that I would have to cancel on her plans. She insisted I still come to her house so that I would not be alone as sick as I was. I could tell then and there she was a caring and compassionate soul. She didn't know how much effort it took for me to mindfully surrender some walls in that moment, to trust the help she was offering. By the time I arrived at her house from work, I was soaked in sweat and doubled over in so much pain I could barely walk. She helped me up to the bathroom, where I locked myself in and stripped off all of my clothes so that the cold tile could cool down my body. I lay in her bathroom like that for hours, crying in excruciating pain. Part of my tears were from the unrelenting discomfort; the remainder were from a broken heart. I was so ill, and I thought for sure if my family were to run to my aid for something, it would be for this. That was not the case though. I had never experienced physical pain and limitations like I had then, and we all have expectations on who should care for us and when. What I neglected to recognize was who God had placed on my path— someone who was a total stranger, who might not have been who I wanted there yet was exactly who I needed.

Edie was gracious and compassionate. She endured my bitter attitude toward her with patience and humility. She could see I was in no condition to move, and instead of asking me questions, she just took charge. I wasn't used to that. I was used to being the one who held it all together for everyone else, to my own detriment much of the time. As hours led to days, Edie didn't fight my stubborn defiance to go to the emergency room; instead, she arranged urgent appointments with the best doctors in the city. Test after test came up negative for anything life threatening. It felt like all of my previous visits to the emergency room, when I went in with excruciating pain and left with a bottle of antacids and a prescription to relax. After several rounds of benign results from more extensive testing, I was given a HIDA scan. It showed that my gallbladder was functioning at 5 percent, practically a dead organ, and needed to be extracted as soon as possible. I had abused my body in more ways than I could think of, leaving me to wonder if this was the punishment for it. Edie remained by my side, making all of the arrangements for surgery without bothering me at all. I had never known someone to be so selfless with me. My family was absorbed in my dad's illness, and my sister and her husband had just had their first child, so I tried to understand their limitations to travel to see me. Nevertheless, it was difficult to accept that nobody came. I had made countless trips down to support and care for them whenever they needed it. It's easy to look back and recognize Edie's heart and indescribably loving actions. In the moment, however, I was not so gracious. Feeling deeply abandoned by the people who were supposed to love me, my resentment manifested in my demeanor toward the one person by my side and caring for me. I spoke to Edie terribly. The bitterness that emerged from my heart displayed nothing of her love and everything of the animosity within me. Not many days pass where I wish I could go back and do that all so differently.

The surgeon opted to remove my gallbladder through my bellybutton, a newer procedural approach at the time. I was too ill to comprehend the risks and side effects of recovery. All I remember was threatening the operating room staff just before they put me under not to mess up. My mother was with Edie in the recovery room when I came to. That was the first time they met, which was incredibly awkward, given Edie introduced herself as my girlfriend. I could see her eventually being like a best friend to me; however, I felt bad making an issue of it, given all she had just done for me. In hindsight, that would have been the most respectful time to address it; I just did not have the mental capacity in the moment to do so.

The first night was horrendous, as the pain in my abdomen was worse than anything I had experienced even prior to the surgery. Turned out the procedure involved some incision to my abdominal muscles, which was not clearly communicated preoperatively. I was not able to tolerate opioid pain medications because they made me extremely nauseous; I remember telling the nurse that during the preoperative process. However, I did not expect to be sent home with nothing to ease my pain. My mother and Edie were my caretakers for that first night. It was kind of nice to hear them talk, perhaps comfort each other in an unexpected way, given the circumstances. It was also nice to hear my mother speak cordially toward Edie. Given she introduced herself as my girlfriend, I was stunned there was no discord.

The next day, my mother explained that it would have been too much a burden on Edie to leave me at my house, so she told her that she would be driving me back south to take care of me at home. Good thing that was what happened, as my recovery was not short at all. Most people are back to normal activity within a week or two of having their gallbladder removed; I could not eat normally, or sit up straight, for that matter, for three months. I had to file for family leave, given the recovery needed. I did some research and found that the complications I was experiencing were similar to others who had the same new approach to gallbladder removal via belly button—particularly the rare case of people who required disruption to the muscle structure, which takes far longer to heal. It was a rough recovery period and simultaneously another green pasture.

Edie got close to my family and even came to visit my dad with me in the hospital on one occasion. I spent the next three months being with my dad as often as I could. He was in isolation for his treatment due to the fact that his immune system was depleted in the stem cell transplant process. I shaved his head when his hair started to fall out and started to care about him in a way I never had before during that season. He was gentle and fragile, handsome and strong. He never once complained about being in pain, nor did he ever complain about the side effects of the treatment. He just kept praising God for the access to such advanced care that promised to save him. He was the most easygoing and compliant patient I had ever seen; every nurse enjoyed checking in on him and loved talking with our family. What could have been and should have been a devastating experience was otherwise filled with enduring hope. Death had left a fresh mark on our family and was threatening to make another stain. The reality of that and the unpredictable illnesses shook up my life. It wasn't until I paused from the rush that I was able to really see it, that I was able to see the preciousness of time and the significance of how we spend it. Up to that point, I had spent every moment trying to quantify life with money and material things, by self-enhancing and self-advancing ways to gain approval from the world. I felt my eyes opening as I realized how vastly I neglected to revere life, as if my eyes previously had scales over them, limiting my vision. I didn't want approval from the world anymore. I wanted it from God. Life, and love, was revealing itself to be significantly more than the physical elements I was focusing on.

I started reading the Bible and talking to God in a new way. I asked him to remove my blindfold, to change the desires of my heart to align with the desires of his heart, and to help me see others the way he sees people. After a few months, I started to feel a sense of overpowering concession filling my entire being. I lost total trust in what I wanted for my life and was beginning to feel a new desire to want to know God and the plans he had for me. I returned to work with a high level of trepidation and an overwhelming decree to flee that life. I was remorseful for choosing my own ways, for redefining right and wrong according to what brought me fairness and solace. The more I read through the scriptures, the more I could feel my eyes opening to the good intentions God had for me, and for all of humanity, for that matter. And I could finally understand how we so easily turn from those ways and the consequences that ensue in the world around us. Quitting my job, or dropping my net, did not make practical sense though. I had a mortgage, a student loan, and a sizable car payment, among other monthly expenses. At the same time, it felt like if I stayed, I was choosing a regrettable path. I wanted what God wanted for my life but was demonstrating a severe lack of trust in how he would bring it about. I think I just expected God to act like a puppeteer; I would give up my life, and in exchange, God would cancel all of my debts and set me free from all of the things holding me down. Ending happily ever after. That wasn't the case, though, at all.

God wasn't a puppeteer. If he was, that would mean he would be the one pulling the strings to do good when he felt like it or allow evil and suffering to ensue equally as so. He would not be a God I would seek out, given the state of the world today, if that was the case. I was starting to understand that he wanted to work *with* me and *for* me, not against me. Yet that was how I had been approaching him for so many years. I prayed with requests for him to do things for me, for him to make things happen or to change people around me so that I could have comfort and peace. All those years, I thought God was ignoring me by not doing exactly what I asked him to do, which in turn spurred my resentment toward him. My approach to God was like my approach to human relationships—controlling and transactional. If someone didn't behave or present the way I thought was best, or if they didn't share the same opinions as I did, I would essentially write them off as simply not fitting into my life. I did the same thing with God. If he didn't agree with my definition of right and wrong, I wrote it off, most notably when it came to scripture. The more I read, the more I could see how the ways I had chosen for my life were the exact ways God warned against. It was one thing to begin to intellectually understand that; it was a whole other to take the first step toward believing it. I felt like I was dying, in the sense that everything I once believed to be true was really not. I felt betrayed by my own self. I struggled to focus, to find purpose and value in anything I was doing anymore.

The industry I was in was also experiencing a turbulent season. The kickbacks and corruption that once controlled how business operated were being exposed faster than anyone could even attempt to cover up. The fact that surgeries could no longer be bought and that surgeons could no longer receive favors for using certain products caused significant decreases in sales and revenue targets. It also forced honest relations and design intentions. The new company I worked for was at one point in time one of the largest players in the industry. The fact that it was being bought out was a shock to everyone, lending to similar vibes to those in the 2008 financial industry. The corporate headquarters for the company acquiring us was in Colorado. I flew out on several occasions to help with portfolio consolidation efforts and new product pipeline definition. I was offered a position to move with the new staff, even assigned a relocation agent to help me shop for a home out there. I was still with Edie at the time, and she loved to snowboard, so we made extended vacations out of the trips. She said that she had always wanted to live out there, so we talked about what that might look like. She even attended all of the work social events associated with the merger, arranging to get to know people and their families before the move. It was the first time ever I was publicly and formally associated with a woman as a spousal partner. And yet that was still not how I saw it in my heart.

I didn't look at her like that, like a spouse or a partner, I mean. I did her hair the night of that one work event like we were just girlfriends getting ready for a party. She was transforming into a best friend kind of companion in my heart. I could barely hug her, in fear of communicating the wrong intention, let alone sleep next to her. It confused and hurt her, to say the least, given her intentions were for more. The resistance in my heart to those desires had started to transform into complete protest. I loved Edie; there was no denying that. I genuinely cared about her well-being and was open to living with her as a companion. I just didn't love her the way she wanted me to, in a romantic, sensual kind of way. Edie was in love with an idea of me, like so many others before her. When we first met, I made all attempts to be honest about my intentions, how I was looking for something much more innocent in a companionship than that of intimacy. In the same vein, I was vulnerable about my sexually sordid past and love of money and power. All of which, unfortunately, she grasped to believe was who I still really was. The more clarity broke down confusion, the more tension that built between us. We began arguing constantly, and not just the bickering type. I was downright belligerent. She was always the one who left relationships, out of fear of abandonment. She left before the potential of being left existed. Naturally, I preyed on that, threatening to leave on a daily basis, actually leaving for a few hours, then returning to keep the vicious cycle alive. Like every other relationship in my life, I was setting the stage for self-destruction.

For about six weeks during our consideration of Colorado, I was paralyzed in grief, living and breathing in the life I had made yet concurrently mourning the nearing end of it. I couldn't get off of the couch, let alone work. I wasn't showing up to meetings and was lying about where I was. I talked to God about my recognition of the violent friction within my soul and how if he wanted me to leave it all, I would. I knelt at my bedside in my room alone at night after work, asking God to speak to me because I needed unmistakable guidance and undeniable direction. I ended each prayer with, "I love you, I believe in you, I have faith in you, and I trust you. Please come into my heart. I am nothing without you. I can do nothing without you." As I was about to close my prayer with that one night, I heard, "You say you love me, yet you do not obey me." I paused the first time I heard it, unsure if what I had heard was in my head or coming from another voice. I had a very quiet home in a very quiet neighborhood. There was no chance of overhearing a neighbor, and I didn't have the television on. I stayed kneeling against the bed, contemplating what I thought I had just heard. Then, for a second, clearer time, I heard, "You say you love me, yet you do not obey me." The voice spoke with gentle authority. I was not afraid of it—I was actually delighted by it. Before I attempted to speak another word, I heard it a third time, more crisp, assuring that it was not in my own head. "You say you love me, yet you do not obey me." I replied, "I know. Give me the courage to leave everything that is separating me from you, because I cannot do it on my own." My brother had also told me to compare anything I heard in prayer or meditation to scripture to test its truth. He had his master's in theology and a pure outlook on life, so I trusted his guidance. I didn't always like it—often hated it, actually. Nevertheless, I searched scripture for the words I had heard and found John 14:15–24, and it convicted my heart in an unmistakable way that night.

The next day when I arrived at work, I sat down to power on my computer to type up my resignation letter. The undeniable courage was present. It happened to be the same day I owed the company a decision about the move to Colorado. I asked my boss for a moment to chat, assuming he thought it was regarding my decision to relocate.

He did not expect me to tell him that I was not only declining the offer but also submitting my resignation. I felt more confident in that discernment than any decision I had ever made in my life. I had no direction, no promised next steps. Just trust and a command. And I felt completely safe with full knowledge that I was not taking the step alone. I still could not comprehend how I would be able to pay my bills, and I knew it was not right to default on anything. So I continued to pray for God to reveal the next steps. Two hours after I submitted my resignation, I received a call from my Realtor. I had listed my house for rent a few weeks prior, thinking I was either going to move to Colorado or potentially move in with Edie. My Realtor had a highly qualified tenant who wanted to move in by the end of the month. The pressure of the mortgage payment was immediately and completely relieved.

I ended up moving in with Edie as I worked to figure out what to do next. She didn't want to just be my friend—she wanted to marry me. Furthermore, she wanted to be a power couple in New York, making a ton of money while proving the world wrong in its limited understanding of love. At one point, that offer of rebellion would have landed well with me. Where was she ten years before? I wondered. And what would have happened if I had gotten an offer like that back then? Despite my disinterest in marriage, I still considered the idea. I was in the process of giving up my home, and I had no idea what stability looked like now. I was selfish, using Edie's desire to be with me as a temporary landing pad from the leap of faith I had just taken. I had never felt such clarity compiled with confusion in all of my life. I had given her a promise ring, which I knew was what sealed the misrepresentation in my intentions. I didn't want to be her wife; I wanted her to be my convenient companion, promising her the same in return. We went out to dinner one night shortly after I decided to move in with her—also after she had given me a ring in a very informal gesture of return the day prior—the dinner being a celebration of sorts. I wasn't sure if it was a celebration or a concession. It was a massive band-style ring with sixty-nine diamonds. The number of diamonds was a reference to sex and my reprehensible past she hoped would resurface in the future. I'm not sure I would have ever found that to be amusing, not even back then. The fact that she gave me something like that led me to see what she really thought of me though. And yet despite all of that, there was an odd sense of comfort in wearing the ring; I can see why so many women are desperate for one. It comes with an idea of forever trust, forever companionship, an idea that you'll never be alone. And being alone happened to be my greatest, growing fear; I accepted the ring because I didn't want to be alone. I also liked the idea of my parents and the rest of the world seeing that my rebellion was not going to be my demise; rather, it would ultimately result in happiness and contentment. Those were my thoughts on the surface anyway. Beneath the surface, the ring was a reminder of a life I wanted absolutely nothing to do with anymore. At dinner, Edie did most of the talking, excited about how much money we would have once our incomes were combined. I had accepted a position with a start-up company as a consultant, providing flexible work hours and generous enough salary while I figured things out. I couldn't hide my lack of enthusiasm, which started another fight between us. All we did was fight about everything; I couldn't figure out why she even wanted to be with me. I wasn't who she wanted me to be, and I wasn't going to eventually turn into that person like she hoped I was. Our fights grew increasingly toxic as she continued to battle my resistance to conform to the idea of love she had in mind. I didn't blame her for being so bitter and resentful. I wasn't what she had signed up for, and I was afraid to tell her the truth. I wanted the acceptance and validation the ring promised; however, I wanted it free from the worldly, conditional obligation it represented.

I was doing some painting in Edie's guest bedroom the following week, trying to pull my weight with house responsibilities, since that also happened to be the room I had been sleeping in while I tried to figure out how to coexist with her. I had taken off the doorknobs to ensure I didn't get any paint on them, since they were antique. She came in to embrace me, saying how much she loved having a home together. I dodged her notion, and another fight started. I was so fed up with it all, with the crushing weight of the lies and pretending to be someone I wasn't. I was also infuriated by the fact that we couldn't just coexist as loyal and committed friends. Why wasn't that enough? Why wasn't that kind of love sufficient? Instead of admitting all of that, I took the antique doorknob in my hand and threw it as hard as I could past her head at the wall. The knob shattered and made a huge hole in the plaster. My heart instantly dropped at the sight of what I had just done—and for what I could have done. I could have hit her in the face. I could have hurt her really badly. She cried in terror and ran out of the house. I cut myself in the process of trying to pick up the broken glass pieces. I went into the bathroom to wash my hands and caught a glimpse of a person I didn't recognize. I stared in the mirror, yet I had no idea who I was. I saw a rebellious, angry, and now violent woman staring back at me. I didn't like the image I saw. I hated myself for hurting Edie the way I had, for emotionally abusing her and now threatening her with physical violence. Something changed within as I tried to recollect the person staring back at me. I encountered burdensome remorse, my eyes slowly opening to my utterly ungodly character. I was a cowardly woman who hid behind alcohol and deceit, emotionally violent and immature, using anger and manipulation to overpower any opposition. I saw a woman who used other women in an egotistical competition against men. I saw a woman staring back at me who represented everything I never wanted to be. I had no idea how it would all fall apart, but it had to. She had to die.

With peace and gratitude,
Chole

Life

Dear Addie, may this note find you well.

All told, I lived with Edie for about three months, departing to stay with my family after that incident. Life started to feel like a series of walls crumbling around me, while I stood as a mere spectator amid the dust and rubble. The person I knew myself to be was dying an apparent and slow death. I closed on a rental agreement for my house and proceeded to pack. I dispersed and donated all of my furniture, and even my clothes and shoes. Of everything about my life in material possessions, I despised my clothes the most. Mainly because I detested the person who wore them. At one point in time, my closet was my favorite room in the house. I had shelves of high heels and organized my shirts and pants neurotically by color. It was a beautiful spring day when my mom came up to help me pack the kitchen. Each plate and glass she lovingly wrapped for potential long-term storage. She was always there for me. When I had the DWI, she drove up on Saturday mornings to take me to see my family, then drove me all the way back on Sunday evenings. When I was determined to go to college, despite everyone else's resistance, she was by my side, supporting my ambitions. She sat through orientation with me and cheered me through to graduation. When I was finished packing up my house, all that was left from a material possession standpoint was a plastic tote of memorable keepsakes, a kayak, and a duffel bag of clothes.

Not a soul on earth could relate to what I was going through. Not even my pastor. I tried talking to my family about what was happening, and while they didn't personally relate, they were the most supportive of this over any other decision I've ever made. My parents always promised that no matter what happened in life, with them we would have a roof over our heads, clothing, and food. I didn't find much value in their forever promise of basic needs until I was no longer able to provide them for myself. I walked away from a six-figure salary, a home in the suburbs of the most powerful city in the world, and dropped all elements of luxury and comfort I had created for myself. Without those things, I felt naked. I literally did not know who I was. My identity was based in what I did, who I knew, and the affiliated highs and lows that came with all of that. To the general eye, I was going through a quarter-life crisis. I was very aware that that was not the case.

Remember that beautiful white Volvo SUV I had, and how much you hated it? You never directly said it, just constantly alluded to how pretentious and unnecessary it was for a single woman to own. Anyhow, the transmission went prematurely, so I traded it in for a small, two-door Volvo sports car that now seemed like a cliché. I drove the I-95 corridor with a tiny car filled with all of my belongings and a kayak on the rooftop. I drove in silence, clueless of what the next hour held for my life, as I could not conceptualize much further beyond the present moment. I wasn't depressed or devastated, if that's what you're thinking. I had never been more sure of anything in my life. I had an absolute and unshakable trust in the process. Nevertheless, there was still a need to grieve in a way. I mourned the loss of my life as I knew it by acknowledging all of the ways it opposed God. I mourned my deliberately selfish choices that used and hurt people, God's fellow image bearers. I mourned how easily and frequently I gave into the alluring conduct that promised to elevate me while disrespecting God's desire for me to walk humbly. I also mourned all of the ways I didn't know God yet attempted to convince myself that my ways were better than his. Above all, I agonized over the sexual sin I had committed, treating the contempt against my own body as common and tolerable to God. Of all my ugly sins, it was the violation against my own body that burdened me the most.

Along the way to my parents, I found myself drawn to pull over at a local grocery store. I hadn't eaten much in weeks, and I was still not hungry, in the way for bodily sustenance, that is. I pulled into a parking spot and sat there, feeling my shoulders droop as my hands still grasped the wheel. The thought of going in to buy bread and wine came to mind, pairing with a desperate hunger for Jesus. His love for humanity convicted my heart in the most gentle and soul-separating way. I was never the type to take criticism well. In fact, it usually caused me to be more defiant, even if it meant spiting myself to prove someone else wrong. And yet, for some reason, the loving wisdom and gentle rebukes against immoral behavior in scripture took hold of my heart in a way nothing else ever had. I walked into the grocery store and purchased a baguette and a bottle of grape juice, foregoing the wine because I was driving. I returned to my car and proceeded to eat the bread and drink the juice, overwhelmed to tears with the deepest sense of gratitude I had ever felt before in my life. Some would say what I did was reckless, especially religious factions. And they would be right to, if God's satisfaction was based on obligatory ritual performance. I searched for Jesus in that meal, with my whole heart, to be my Savior. I searched for the perfect human, the one who withstood the punishment for *my* thoughtless choices. Just because I didn't like the sound of deserving death for my actions didn't mean it wasn't true. I had completed catechism classes and all of my holy sacraments. Never once, in decades of partaking in that meal, did I know what it truly meant to eat and drink of it. Because it wasn't until then that I realized the just punishment I deserved for the way I was living my life. I recall thinking in that moment—I didn't want to die. I knew at that point that there was absolutely nothing I could do of my own accord to make things right between me and God—I needed Jesus. I needed the punishment he took, the death I deserved for the actions derived from my hard and prideful heart, to overtake my heart. I swallowed the body and tasted the blood, and an overpowering sense of peace that surpassed understanding surged through my entire being.

I wanted more of that abiding sense of peace and love, so I started a new daily routine at my parents' house of reading the Bible. Starting with the Gospel of Matthew and the Old Testament book of Isaiah, I set a chair outside early in the morning and read for almost an hour, in company of the sunrise. Then I would go about my day, doing some consulting work and making a more authentic effort in relationship with my family. When evening came, I took my chair back outside and sat for another hour, in company of the sunset, listening in the quietude for God's voice. I read to get to know God, then opened my heart to invite anything at all he had to say to me. The routine was completely contradictory to my former relationship with God. I went from resisting scripture to running to it. From resisting God's ways to wanting to them etched on my heart.

Things with Edie weren't over, despite my moving out and living over two hours away. In fact, she came down to visit often, as she had the flexibility since she worked from home. The office I consulted with was in proximity to my parents', which bothered Edie a lot, given her heart was tied to zip codes more prestigious, particularly those in the New York area. I told her I wanted to be close to my family, given everything that was going on, and would not consider moving back north with her. In addition to my father's illness, my mother had suffered a stroke. I watched as it happened, as her face started to droop while we were talking on the sun porch one late afternoon. She said she was fine and did not want to go to the hospital, and there was nothing I could do to force her beyond her own will. Just a couple of hours later, the symptoms became worse, painful, and, in some cases, irreversible. She was left with residual numbness on the left side of her body, mainly in her hand. I think she was very fortunate, given the amount of time that passed after the first sign. I was all too familiar with that level of stubbornness, so who was I to judge?

Edie spent a lot of time with my family, a wall I had never before let down. I could tell she was growing more and more bitter toward me and the changes in my desires for life. It was hard not to appreciate the effort she was making, which inevitably led to more confusion for me. During one of her visits, she asked me to make a dream board with her of pictures of all the things we wanted. She posted images of beautiful homes, a Porsche, a boat, and a family wearing NY sports attire. I didn't know how to tell her that I didn't want any of that or how meaningless all of those things were to me now. Even her idea of family had a worldly identity to it. I wish I'd had the courage to tell her that my feelings had nothing to do with her. She was lovable and beautiful, and I wish I could have had the chance to love her in a purer sense. She couldn't understand the love I was searching for. Not many people could, especially how intimate love could exist without sex. That was the love I always wanted to be though. The idea of love that peaked with romance would have meant we were all designed to find one human being and share deep, unconditional love with that one person forever, giving full devotion to that one person, our whole hearts and selves. That same version then meant that love was exclusive to those who found it, or to those who didn't find it to define their own version of it. Despite my hardened, vengeful heart, I always believed in Jesus's command to love one another as we loved ourselves. To love all people, the way we would perhaps only consider cherishing the one we choose to. An impossible feat without a new heart. Another rotten root in my heart led to the fact that I did not love myself—I didn't even like myself enough to respect myself. I didn't want romantic love that was secluded to one other human being. I wanted a heart that loved all human beings, with a deep and unconditional desire to serve them. I wanted to experience a higher love and a greater fellowship with humanity, other than that which was man-made.

It was clear that my time with Edie had to come to an end. I didn't want to hurt her, yet I also had no idea how to get out of my relationship with her without doing so. She was so good to me. On a daily basis, she just wanted to work together through life. She genuinely wanted to make me happy, as she defined happiness. For my thirtieth birthday, she rented out a beach house on a private island for us and my family. As if that wasn't enough, she rented out her home near Manhattan, then rented a home near my parents' in hopes that this thing I was going through was temporary. It all happened so fast, one thing after another. The kinder she was to me, the harder it was to tell her the truth. I tried my hardest not to be part of the home rental decision because I knew I was not able to take responsibility for it. It was a twenty-five-hundred-square-foot home with a price tag well beyond my affordability now. I explained to her that I was not able to contribute financially, and she insisted on it being her way of supporting me. I said no in every way, except firmly and directly. She stayed up north while I worked on getting the house ready for her. Things like resurfacing the kitchen cabinets and painting the walls, cosmetic-upgrade attempts to help make it feel more like hers. My life choices were becoming real at that point. I was preparing to make a home with someone, the thought of which was previously a game to me. I didn't take talk like that seriously with anyone, just like I didn't take talks of commitment seriously. I used words that alluded to those things to keep people close for as long as I needed them, but I had no real intentions of following through. Well, this wasn't a game anymore. There was a home, a physical address, with my name synonymously attached to it with someone else's.

Edie came down the third weekend to make arrangements for cable and utilities. Her absence had almost made me feel like I could make it work, at a distance. However, when I saw her, it reminded me that she was a real person, not a comfortable companion in cyber-text space interested in being a digital pen pal. She was a real person, making real—significant—changes to her life in an effort to compromise with mine. That weekend, we were sitting in the living room, her on the couch and me on the floor next to the coffee table. I was designing a website to expand my consulting work, immersed in the messaging I was trying to convey. I was having a difficult time focusing on what I wanted to sell. It was hard to type with that big ring on my left hand. I felt sick to my stomach selling myself out for worldly affinity. Falling so easily in love with money, seeking it as my savior for acceptance and worth. Making countless cowardly moral bargains, allured by lies to prove love conquered all by repelling male chauvinism and an institutional definition of a selective God. These were the thoughts the ring triggered, blocking me from any level of productive thought. Edie got up to go to the kitchen, candidly frustrated with my distant daze. As soon as she was out of the room, I heard a voice. It said, "The path you're on is a literal path to death." I recognized the voice as the one I had heard by my bedside months before. I froze in place, not knowing what to do with it. I sat in what felt like a pause in time, hearing the message again, only more crisp the second time. Edie returned to the room, and in an effort to avoid any awkwardness, I hastily rushed to click the button that would make my website live. Edie saw what I did and said, "What are you doing?! Why wouldn't you wait for me? We are in this together, and this is a big moment!" I didn't consider her in my decisions, and I didn't think it was a big deal at all. Frustrated, she went back into the kitchen to fix our plates for dinner. Once again, the voice spoke: "The path you're on is a literal path to death." It spoke with loving authority, which my heart desired to obey. I could not lie anymore, and I certainly could not hypocritically commit myself to Edie under God. The choice was clear, and it was time to choose: life or death.

The following day, Edie went back to her home up north, and I continued working on the new house, painting in the bedroom. The ceilings were stunningly high, so I was up on a ladder, hoping to find some peace in the quiet, gentle strokes. To the contrary, as I worked my way around the room, anxiety began to grow. My soul was stirring with disturbance as I painted the room Edie expected us to sleep in together. That was wrong; there was no more confusion about it. And I couldn't lie about it anymore, to myself or anyone else. I came down from the ladder and fell to my knees on the floor. I cried in a way that felt like my whole body was weeping. Only one word came into my mind, out of my heart, and past my lips with a desperate cry: "Abba! Abba, help. Abba … help." I had never said that word before, nor did I know where it had come from within me. I felt a sense of peace and comfort come over me, and I stopped crying as I stood up. I took a break and went out to the store to purchase some home goods like hand towels and mugs, to make Edie feel loved in the space. I was completely and peacefully detached, with a strong knowing that I was not going to be living in that home after that night. My focus was on making the home as beautiful as I possibly could for her. The last thing I did was fill the refrigerator with her favorite foods and the counter with her favorite coffee and snacks. I left a note that said, "I love you, please know that."

I went to my parents' that night and slept on the only couch spared from the recent demolition. I lay there in the dark, begging God to do something. I confessed that I did not have the courage to leave Edie, yet I wanted so badly to follow in his ways. Just as I was about to lie down, my phone beeped, and it was a text message from Edie. She started with an apology for the late message, then said she was sorry, but she couldn't do it. She could not make the move, and she did not believe in where I was going with my life. She wanted money, she wanted intimacy in the form of sex, she wanted a wife and kids, and she could see that I wasn't going to give her any of that. My heart was overjoyed with gratitude to God for intervening, for hearing my cry. I cried to my heavenly father for help, I admitted my weakness, and he became my strength. Edie gave me two days to collect all of my belongings from the house. I did just that, and we never spoke again.

I brought my duffel bag to my sister and brother-in-law's house and ended up sleeping on their couch in their basement for the next eighteen months while I figured out what came next. That's around the time you reached out. It had been over three years since we last spoke. You sent me an email, asking if I was married and traveling the world. How far I was from the person you thought you knew, and how delighted I was to divulge that I was not married or occupying the life you thought I was. I don't think I was ever so glad to see your name in my inbox. You made my soul smile. That was the longest we had gone without contact, and I didn't think I would ever get the chance to tell you the truth, yet here was the open door to do just that. Then you emailed with your phone number, just in case I had deleted it from my phone. I called you, and to my surprise, you answered, happily at that. I don't think I had ever before heard you happy either. Most times we spoke, you sounded obliged and distant. When we finally met up for dinner, that was when I could see that there was something so different about you. A radiant kind of beauty and a change in your eyes that seemed to be shining directly from your heart. I still carried the conviction I had about you from the day we met, which led me to be more confused than ever about our relationship, given all that I had just experienced. I loved hearing about the impact you were having with your work, the service you did for others, and perhaps even more so how you had started your own search for God. I wanted to tell you everything I had just experienced, except I didn't know how just yet. It was still happening, and I didn't know how to describe it. I was in the process of being transformed, which sounds a bit bizarre saying out loud, especially to someone you haven't seen in years. It felt so surreal sitting across the table from you, seeing you through these different eyes, with a love more innocent than ever for you. Speaking of, remember those teddy bears from Europe I gave you that night? For the life of me, I cannot remember the brand. Anyway, I kept them for you. Through multiple moves, breakdowns, and breakups. You always talked about how much you wanted them, but you thought they were too expensive. So, I had them special-ordered for you for Christmas the year we stopped talking again. And I held onto them, in the event I ever saw you again. It was like carrying a piece of you with me over those years. I wonder if you still have them.

I'm telling you now what I should have told you that night. Instead of talking to you about transitioning from corporate life into entrepreneurship, I wish I would have told you that I met Jesus. That I had dropped everything I knew in life to follow him. That I was not wealthy, and I didn't have a home in a reputable zip code anymore or a noble job title to identify with. What I wanted to tell you was that I was happy, for the first time in my life. I was content with unexplainable peace, living in my sister's basement, on a journey completely fueled by faith. Despite how grateful I was to see you and to be talking the way we were, I still had scars that made me weary of trusting you enough to be so vulnerable. That's a reflection of me, not you. I was afraid to be completely honest, which at the time I didn't realize meant I was still seeking something from you—your approval of me.

Faith was really all I had. I wrote a new priority list: God, family, work, in that order. I was disciplined in sticking to my morning and evening routine with God and working on building healthier relationships with my family. As for work, I wasn't sure what I really wanted. I had a mentor review my website, as I was not getting many inquiries. He asked me to think more about what I wanted to do because he thought my website was looking more like a nonprofit cause than a business service. I explained to him how I wanted to combine servant leadership with my global business experience somehow. The process was frustrating for us both. I was growing impatient with the fact that I was running out of money and about a week away from bills being due. I was in the kitchen at my parents', cooking lunch, when my dad walked in to ask how I was doing. I snapped. I told him that I was angry at God for leading me to leave everything, knowing I had bills to pay and basic needs, yet here I was with nothing left. I had no home, no steady work, no name for myself. Nothing to show for my life. My dad told me to have patience, that everything was going to work out. I cried as he left the room, then proceeded to scream at God. And I mean I screamed. I shouted uncontrollably, demanding that he tell me what else he could possibly want from me. I had dropped everything to follow him and was left with exactly $1.16 in my bank account. In a month, I had $1,786 in bills due. When I finished my complaining, I took a deep breath and once again felt an unexplainable and undeserving sense of peace overcome me. I was online later that night, searching for leads for work, when I received a live inquiry message about my consulting services. It turned into a job offer that paid double my monthly expenses. I received my first check the day before my bills were due. God had provided; he had never planned to leave me. His timing was just not my timing. He wanted me to trust. I was starting to understand the difference between religion and relationship. And that God, through Jesus, was after the latter.

My brother eventually pitched in to my cause and bought me a queen-size air mattress so that I could have a more normal sleep situation in a bed. The lack of judgment and amount of love my family showed me was greater than any amount of money, title, or material possession I had ever had or could want. I adjusted my evening routine by joining the local health club. After spending so many years abusing my body with lust and gluttony, the draw to a new season of nourishment for my body, mind, and spirit was fitting. The discipline and structure helped me too. At the end of each workout, I sat in the sauna with God. Some nights, I would talk; others, I would just listen. I did that every single night at the same time, leaving at 10:00 p.m. for one more stop to the grocery store. It was quiet and peaceful in the market that time of night, and a stroll through the aisles offered some nostalgia and humility. I used to food shop on a daily basis, spending superfluous amounts of money on food for myself without ever looking at the cost. If someone had asked me how much a gallon of milk cost, I couldn't have told them. I was starting to understand how Mom-Mom felt all those years before, going from being able to buy whatever you wanted to only being able to afford the bare necessities. I couldn't afford to shop like that anymore, and I didn't find it limiting at all. I found great pleasure in a simple stop for a nectarine. That's all I would purchase, one nectarine. It was a generous do-over and a relearning of the role of money.

Shortly after reconnecting with you, I received another blast from the past: Lee. Of all people, I never, ever would have expected to hear from her again. Five years after her emotional assault, she was asking to see me—begging and pleading at my every objection. Her friend who had left me the threatening phone calls years before added to the barrage of messages, asking me to be willing to see her again. I eventually obliged, mainly because I wanted to see how my newly transformed heart would respond. When I arrived at her house, I actually felt excited to see her, hopeful that perhaps it was a new chapter and we would talk about being friends again. Unfortunately, that wasn't the case. She wanted something else, and after five years of silence, I couldn't believe that was why she had called me so randomly. I told her no, multiple times, and actually felt bad because I could see her from new eyes. She sought sex to feel beautiful, to feel acceptance … and she didn't know that sex was not necessary to get that from me. I gave her a strong hug, grasped her face in my hands, looked her softly in the eyes, and told her how beautiful she was. I asked her to stop doing this to herself, to cherish her body and stop allowing others to violate the preciousness of it. In the past, I would have compromised myself in order to please someone else, and now I was confident that was not sacrificial love. I felt a shield of armor around my heart that I had not ever felt before, where in the face of known temptation, my spirit was impenetrable. She returned my gaze and said nobody had ever made her feel as loved or as beautiful as I did. I hugged her goodbye, knowing that was the final time I would see her. I got into my car feeling confident in my no and grateful for Jesus's compassionate love. I still miss her though. Memories of Lee are a constant reminder to me of life under the sun, and love's ultimate mission still in progress.

We had just reunited after three years, so I didn't think it would have helped to share any of that with you. I had hopes for a new chapter for us and wanted to stay focused on that. If I close my eyes, I can still see you sitting next to me at dinner that night after we went shopping at the outlets. Sitting on the curved edge of the round table we were seated at, sharing my menu, with the most puzzled of looks on your face. I tried to stay focused on the menu, because I was completely content with the day and really did not want to know what was on your mind. Maybe because I subconsciously knew, and I didn't want it to be true. You pulled my menu down and asked when you thought we would take the next step. We had been talking for just a couple of months after years of silence, and all I wanted was pure friendship and a companion to serve God with. I was enjoying going to church with you and taking Sunday adventures, growing convinced that that was the convicting purpose for our connection I'd been trying to pinpoint since I first met you. Why else would we have reconnected at that point in time? Except your idea of a next step in our relationship was sex. A familiar old feeling of confusion and disappointment returned. All those years, I just wanted to love you. Except you never felt love from the poison and deceit I had fed you. That was the whole reason I even started searching for God—so that I could truly love you! Money, status, and power could not buy the acceptance and inner peace the depth in your eyes silently cried out for. Every attempt at loving you consistently led to contention, and true love does not lead to that. Love was a word I once disgracefully traded for lust, and I was familiar with that public enemy now. The one disguised as an imposter, promising gratifying happiness in exchange for soul deprivation. I wanted so badly to find out how to love you truly and purely that I was willing to die to my own life to find it. How do you tell someone that? Clearly, I didn't know how, or else I wouldn't be writing to you now all these years later.

I avoided answering you directly in an effort to buy more time. I'd say I regret that; however, if I told you the truth at that point in time, we probably would not have made it to Iceland. I remember feeling guilty about how I had dodged your question about sex with a "if that's what's supposed to happen, then it will happen" kind of flighty response. My yes was not yet my yes, and my no was not yet my no, a lesson in how indecision is still a decision. My irresoluteness led you to think I might have had some interest in a different kind of relationship with you, and I did not realize then just how wrong that was. I was still focused on exposing the fraudulent definitions of love more than I was on just merely loving, without having control of the consequences. I allowed you to think I wanted to be with you and that it was just a matter of time before I fully committed. I spent so much time blaming you for the lack of trust between us that I didn't even consider that I was part of the problem. Everyone who knew me through you thought that I was the kindest, gentlest, most gracious person on earth, while everyone who knew you through me thought that you were shifty, confusing, and dishonest. I painted you out to be a horrible person, while you painted me to be a saint. It's hard for me to sit here and confess this to you now, knowing just how deeply I hurt you, while I played myself out to be a misunderstood, innocent victim. I strung you along for years, with an idea of magical, unconditional love. As if you needed me to show you the way to it. I acted like I was some savior of love to you when, in fact, it was I who needed saving.

If that wasn't evident to me yet, it became so. You watched as my peace and fulfillment drifted slowly into discontented discouragement again. It was hard to make sense of that, given my active, reconciling relationship with God. I had a successful workflow moving with my consulting business and even met my previous year's salary, which was pretty good, given I was new to independent contract work. I had built relationships with major partners and established a network of business opportunities within the first eight months of launching, including assuming the chief executive officer position of another start-up. But you remember all of that; I was working a lot from your apartment at the time. God, family, work; I thought I was doing everything right, and I could not understand why I was still so unhappy. Nothing you did could change how I felt, and while it clearly didn't show, I was grateful for every attempt you made. From baking me my favorite breakfast treats to just inviting me to spend time with you. I was so excited to take on a real adventure together and to really just get away from everything that reminded me of my former self.

The idea of taking a trip like that, for personal reasons, was exciting as well. I had been to a lot of places in the world, for work, alone. I didn't really know what it would be like to explore a foreign land with someone else. I shared my travel experiences with my siblings and family, sending them tons of pictures and calling them to tell stories of incredible sights or simple nuances. It always felt too marvelous for just my eyes to see. I wanted to share those experiences with others, to see the amazement in other people's eyes. I suppose this was also the chance to do that.

Two days before we were scheduled to leave, I had been asked to be the keynote speaker at a start-up networking event. The topic was how to successfully transition your career from corporate America to entrepreneurship. I invited Emma to come with me because she had always asked about what I was doing. Our relationship was also strained. I had spent the past two years with Edie, leaving little time for anyone else. If time did present itself, I declined because I didn't want to be in a bar or drinking in general. This was my attempt to build a new bridge, to set new boundaries in an effort to introduce her to who I really was. We arrived early, and as were walking toward the venue she asked what I was planning to speak about. My hand was just inches from the door handle when she said it. I turned to respond, suddenly baffled, and said, "I actually don't know."

In the matter of a single moment, I had lost any and all professional intelligence. It was like someone had erased my brain. All of the strategies I had accomplished, certified knowledge I had acquired, and experience I had attained were gone. Deleted. Unavailable. We walked in, and the host quickly ran up to greet us. She directed Emma toward the bar area and asked if I needed to set up for a PowerPoint presentation or anything. I didn't know what to say, and I didn't want to let her down. I told her that I thought something supernatural had just happened to me because I had literally forgotten everything I once knew about the subject. She gave me an odd look and asked if I could still give it a try. I ended up giving a very brief talk on the courage required to follow your heart, the risks and losses it takes, and the significance of *how* you perform your work in comparison to *what* you can achieve. About twenty minutes into what should have been a forty-five-minute talk, I told everyone that they should probably go to the bar and get a drink. A woman from New York, who Emma had been talking to, approached me after the crowd dispersed to introduce herself. Her name was Thea. She told me a bit about herself, then abruptly shifted the conversation, asking me if I could pray for her. Finding her inquiry extremely odd, I engaged further since the night was revealing all sorts of unexpected surprises already. We talked some more, and then she confessed that she felt a prompting to speak with me about ministry and that I should consider that as my path forward. I would not have believed the things that happened to me that night if I had not personally lived them. We exchanged contact information, as I told her I was leaving town for a bit, for Iceland. She told me to text her when I returned to let her know what I found there. Emma and I drove her to the train station, then took a very quiet ride home. I didn't know how to share out loud what had all just happened to me.

After I dismissed the notion of being in a romantic relationship with you, I guess I should have expected another breakup of sorts. I wanted you intimately in my life without being romantically intimate with you. That level of love wasn't enough for you though, and I was fighting a resistance to respect that. We were on such opposite sides of the definition of love that it made it impossible to even be friends. I could understand how confusing I made things. I didn't even blame you for not wanting to be around me after that. Once again, that old familiar notion of your rejection had returned. Except this time I didn't feel rejected. I wasn't crushed or devastated. I was not confused. I was confident I was not who you wanted me to be. Though I was hopeful you would give me another chance, I never would have expected you to act the way you did on that trip. I wanted to put feelings aside, be practical adults about a commitment we had made together, and just focus on taking an adventure in a foreign land. It was on your bucket list, after all, and even after I offered my ticket for you to take someone else, you insisted you wanted to go with me. I did my best to focus on the unknown and leave any animosity behind. The moment I arrived to pick you up for the airport, I knew we were in for a rough week together. You barely spoke a word to me, let alone showed any interest in what we were about to do. In my attempt at excitement for the trip the night before, I started looking up quotes about travel and came across this one by Neeraj Narayanan that I will never forget: "If you want to know a person, travel with him. If you want to know him in and out, climb a mountain with him. Go up a mountain with him for seven days. See how he speaks of the skies and the earth. By the time you come down, you might love each other a lot more, or you might never want to know each other again. The mountains teach you a lot." Little did I know just how much wisdom lay ahead in that statement.

Within the first two days, we explored the wonders of the Blue Lagoon and then walked for hours, in silence, through the city of Reykjavik in the snow. Barely a handful of words exchanged over the course of forty-eight hours amid breathtaking sights of dramatic landscape. I already didn't want to know you anymore. We were strangers with memories, confined in a tiny Airbnb without cell service or cable television. Conversation with each other was literally all we had. I remember staring at you above my book at night as you read your Kindle in your own little world. I woke up on the third day and decided that you were not going to ruin that trip for me, that I was not alone—I had God—and I was going to use the quietude to continually seek him. That plan fit well with our proximity to Hallgrímskirkja. That's where I ended up when I went out for walks alone. I sat there and prayed as the crowds of tourists came in and out. I heard the local Icelandic church choir practice, delighted when the children had their turn to sing their songs. We were there during Holy Week, which again was unplanned yet ever so fitting. I took one book along with me, *Rediscover Jesus* by Matthew Kelly, and a booklet of prayers of surrender. So much time I spent during that trip in prayer, asking God to teach me what it meant to surrender. I kept seeing that word in scripture and was meditating on Jesus's teachings on rebirth. I had given away all of my belongings and sought his ways over my own; however, there was still something missing, making me feel like I was only half-committed. The morning of the fifth day, we took that tour of the southern coast. I was mildly terrified when we pulled up to what appeared to be an empty field of volcanic ash and desert-like brush. No signs of human life at all, and we were all asked to exit the bus. A storm was rolling through, winds like we've never felt and hail pelting our heads. Our target was a hole in the ground, which led to an underground cave formed by a lava stream thousands of years ago. You walked in without hesitation, while I paused for a moment to acknowledge the shovel that marked the entry spot. I asked the guide what the shovel was for, and he replied, "In the event we get snowed in." Needless to say, I didn't want to proceed. I was also unable to control how disturbed I felt by your utter ability to shut me out, even during a glacier climb—how many times do you climb a glacier in your life? You talked to complete strangers as if they were your best friends and treated me as if I were invisible.

I prayed during the rides to each site, asking God to intervene and make his love known on that trip. As we continued exploring, I felt a sense of separation from you, an emotional weight lifting and freeing me from feeling any sort of responsibility for your behavior. It opened room in my heart to appreciate the most spectacular aspects of God's creation I had ever seen. Boiling water coming from the geysers in the ground, wild ponies roaming the hills, black sand beaches, sea lions, and magnificent backdrops of waterfalls and small homes with moss and goats on the rooftops. The beauty in the landscape was so natural and peace filled it felt fake. Mountains predating the tenth century, basalt columns, and jagged sea stacks. Our feet walked the Reykjanes Peninsula—we walked on tectonic plates that connect Eurasia and North America, for goodness sake. I've never experienced a day like that in my life, or one like it since. Especially what happened next— when my life changed forever. I don't remember why we separated; I just remember heading for the edge of the cliff to the right of the church of Vik. I found myself there alone, not another soul within eyesight.

The sky in front of me was split in a unique way, with thicker clouds forming a veil-like cover over the water, and bright blue sky spread across the land. The only sounds were of the waves connecting with the sea wall beneath my feet and the seagulls swarming above. To my left in the very far distance was a snow-peaked mountain range, and in front of me was nothing but the sea as far as the horizon stretched. I stood in awe of it, reflecting on the day and taking in the sounds of the birds above and ocean below. I started to think about all of my prayers from that week, and I wanted answers. Everything God made was so beautiful, so good. Here I was in the midst of it, in the most naked and natural of ways, with a discontent heart. I had been asking God all week what it meant to surrender, and I came to an abrupt realization that I was still living after my own plans. A comfortable commitment to God where I sat with him twice a day, and in between, I went about my business according to how I thought best. I hadn't given my life to God; I had left one plan for my life and created another, even though I thought I was doing it for him. Except God didn't need anything from me; his desire was for my heart. Not for me to necessarily start a business or make plans that were again dependent on my own accord. He wanted me to be in a dependent relationship with him. He wanted me to trust his will for my life, which was to make me a new human by reconciling my life with his. I was angry for how my life was going, yet again, and I blamed God for it. I told myself that I enjoyed what I was doing, except I didn't. I enjoyed what my actions portrayed on paper. It was bold and risky to leave a stable income and make it on your own. I wasn't doing it for God though. I was focused on money, again, not trusting God to provide and still seeking identity in my own ways. I figured I would have God in my life, which would make me good, in addition to a self-made business with a purer approach. I wanted God and money. I wanted to be good while still seeking all the comforts the world had to offer. I compartmentalized God, half-heartedly committing my life to him. He was still just something good in my life, rather than the absolute attainment of my life. With a contrite heart, I turned my face toward the sky and apologized, repenting from new depths of my soul.

In that moment, the world fell silent. I could no longer hear the ocean clap or the birds speak. I could still see the movement of it all; I just could not hear it. I felt instantly afraid, and then just as instantly, the fear was replaced with peace and calm. I realized then the authority of the quietude. I looked up and said, "You have my attention. If you have something to say to me, please say it." I heard, "I have good intentions for your life." When I heard that, I was overcome with a desire to glorify God, replying, "Take it all: my ideas, my plans, my ways. I trust you. All I want to do is glorify you, with my life and my words, with my thoughts and my actions." Just then, I felt a loving sensation enter into the top of my head, filling my entire being down into my toes. I received a wholehearted desire to fall to my knees in the presence of such inordinate, merciful love. I asked, "What should I do now?" To which I heard, "Testify." The sounds of the world gently returned. I didn't want to leave that spot or the powerful, protecting presence of love, but I wasn't sure how long I had been there, so I had no choice but to walk away to make sure I still had a ride back to town. I started to walk down the mountain side and ran into you. I remember how excited I was to tell you what had just happened! I told you to go and listen to the silence! You stood there for a minute and looked around, with an expression on your face as if I were insane. Meanwhile, I felt like I was floating on air. I felt so light. I wish you could have felt it. I wish you could have experienced what I just had.

When we got back on the bus, you turned to me, saying, "You look different. How do you feel?" Quite a thought-provoking question, especially after almost a week of silence. Without much thought, I replied, "Free. I feel free." I didn't have any other words to describe how I felt. To describe the release from an oppressively heavy weight. As we started to drive away, I kept my eyes fixed on the sky. I felt like a criminal who had been sentenced to life in prison, who just received release without penalty or charge. Who the Son sets free is free indeed.

With peace and gratitude,
Chole

True Love

Dear Addie, may this note find you well.

That whisper I heard in my childhood bedroom, now thirty years ago, was the first time I ever heard Satan's voice. It was subtle, rational, and most of all responsive to my pleas in the circumstances. Much like Eve in the garden, I welcomed the suggestive tone and permitted it to penetrate my heart, causing me to doubt God's care for me and his faithful authority over all of creation. I think it was so easy to doubt God back then because I had no clue who he was. I knew *of* God, *of* Jesus, and *of* the Holy Spirit, yet I had no relationship with them. Only a religious comprehension of God spoken through the lens of institutional pride, conditional character, and distant affiliation. In that young moment, my heart was desperate for a version of love that would incite an instant gratification of peace and reconciliation. And because that did not happen, the way I wanted it to, when I wanted it to—I forswore it. I felt used by God, ashamed for having faith in him while he sat silently as I wept in heart-shattering ache. That voice would later suggest that God was not dependable, that everything I needed to instill peace and protection in my life was within my own grasp. I've heard stories from my parents and relatives about my childhood, specifically of how when asked what I wanted to do when I grew up, my response was "I'm going to make the money." And that's exactly what I did. I actually went a step further and idolized it as the savior to all of life's challenges.

I couldn't understand the point of Christianity in America, if its purpose was an obligation to institutional church membership and a semblance of love that delivered people into divided groups resembling one another's opinions, characteristics, and interests. Love that was overpowered by diversity, afraid of gender equality, and far too resistant to obey anyone—let alone God. I needed to know there was real justice in this world, that it had the power to flood my purview and set things right. I needed to know that love was more than fleeting emotions and appeasing ceremony. I needed to know that peace was real and obtainable, that when paired with love was unshakeable—regardless of circumstance. I guess the time between those impassioned thoughts and now could be looked at as life in the wilderness. A time filled with confusion, arrogance, and shame. All of my decisions were based on my own desires, my own will for my life, and my own understanding in all circumstances. Where the array of emotions that accompanied that logic acted as the barometer between success and failure.

I was an angry child, galvanized by life's hardships, who grew up to be an arrogant, impassioned adult. And I don't blame anyone for that. Everyone at some point in life experiences trauma; it's an inevitable reality in this life, presently under the sun. When I first started reading scripture, one of the most profound points of clarity I had was hearing Jesus say that he was not leaving us in a safe place. He warned that we would experience trouble. I had been walking through life angry at God for claiming he had control over the world while it was still filled with violence and suffering. The thing is, Jesus never claimed that once he came, the world would be instantly made right. There was more work to be done on earth yet, work that required our contribution, with help and comfort from his spirit. In the same tone of transparency toward trouble, Jesus reassured us that he had already overcome the source of all our troubles. He has overcome illness, addiction, blame, loneliness, rejection, inadequacy, poverty, even death. And any other element within the universe that threatens to destroy pure and perfect love. I never gave much thought to my role in all of that as a human. I never considered how the words I spoke, or the decisions I made, the thoughts I thought, or the actions I took had any impact on the cruelty, hardship, and divide that still exists. It was easier to blame God, the one in charge. It was easier to think God messed up, that God made some mistakes when he created me and he needed to own that. It was also easy to blame other people and expect them to tolerate my poor behavior in the process. That it was on them if they could not accept me for who I was. That's what was so appealing about masks; they hid the pain of injustice, brokenness, and disgrace.

When I look back at old pictures of myself, I see a battle-worn woman who used makeup as war paint and elegant material possessions as diversions to hide what she really thought about her self-worth. I was obsessed with justice because of all of the injustice I had experienced in my life. Repayment defined by my own standards, which was dominance over anything and anyone who attempted to suppress me. Eventually, God became the obscure figure relative only in philosophical thought, inaccessible and impractical for everyday survival. A heart sitting in such posture, burdened by betrayal and provocation from the people supposed to love and protect it the most, can only approach life in one way: defensive conflict. Deaf to discipline, rebellious against lawfulness, and relentlessly arrogant in pursuit of self-defined peace. I made a choice to live independent of God, as a misunderstood member of his church, in an effort to prove in my own way that *my* version of love conquered all. I built a military of his very people, the humans he created in his likeness, as pawns in the game that was my life. My mission was to declare battle against the exclusive, elusive version of love I knew to be God's, and the people who practiced the same. I could not believe in a God whose people lived out their lives in utter selfishness, placing themselves above all, abusing their children, fighting in constant discord, defined by their material possessions and societal status, all the while divided by their varying notions of who the God was they all supposedly believed in. People were confusing and unfaithful. They didn't care that they hurt me, so I didn't care if I hurt them. I loved people who loved me and destroyed anyone who even remotely offended me.

The one common theme that had the power to permeate all the cynicism, doubt, and disbelief was love. The undercurrent that attempted to define love while perpetually seeking the true definition of it. That was what I needed to uncover. I needed to know that love was legitimately unifying, that it could turn real hate into incorruptible peace. I needed to know that love could feed the hungry and house the poor. I needed to know that the forgiveness associated with love was not conditional, that it was accompanied by merciful and transformative power that vulnerably desired good. That's where you came in.

When I met you, I saw sadness in your eyes. A confident, arrogant exterior shell with layers of masks that hid the shame and pain you carried within. I wanted to take that away, to love you so purely and truly that you could see what I saw—an innocent child, created out of love, undeserving of the critical and confusing forms of love you came to know. In many ways, I wanted to save you from yourself, from the self-destructive choices that promised happiness yet consistently guaranteed disappointment. I wanted to save you from being hurt, from walking paths that I could see were not good for you. I wanted to be a place of safety for you, a place where you could be broken absent of humiliation and guilt. I wanted to be the one who didn't judge you and just welcomed you in. I wanted to be everything for you, in hopes that in return it would be everything for me. There was always a catch, and you knew it. That's why you stayed within the bounds of one-night stands and short-lived relations, never getting too close to where something would be required from you. You wanted the freedom to come and go, the freedom to behave however you wanted and be accepted for exactly that. You wanted to consume and leave, then return and refuel. What you were asking for was a version of love that was volatile and afraid, disguised as unconditional and valiant. I wanted that version of love too at one point, until the last day I saw you. I looked at you with new eyes and realized I was looking into a mirror all those years. Your reflection was characteristic of my own, and in a strange attempt to save you, I realized I was the one seeking a savior.

This is the final letter. Each of these stories has exposed to you the truth in my secret heart, to which I've kept nothing hidden. I have not lied to you. I have vulnerably unmasked myself in order for you to know the truth, so that by it you might gain understanding. By the conclusion of this last letter, you will have been fully exposed to my unadulterated heart, in all its brokenness and reconstruction. What you know now, my dear Addie, is that for all of the years you knew me, I was a fraud of a human. I lied to you and to everyone, intentionally consuming others to avoid taking responsibility for my flawed choices. I sold my soul for acceptance and pursued money as my savior, while offering my body as a rebellious prop for power. What was always true, as clouded and confused as it was, was my love for you. I just didn't know how to say it, or live it, without it being correlated to romantic affection. So I did everything I possibly could to prove it, my own way. And in that process, I became the monster I originally wanted to defeat.

I did anything for love, except obey and revere it. I loved money, which made it impossible to love God. I worshiped unforgiveness and my own definitions of justice and vengeance, making it impossible to embrace God's authority. I contributed to a broken world while claiming to be a victim of its hateful and hurtful ways. I was a hypocrite in the grandest sense and will be grateful for all of eternity for having my eyes and ears opened to see and hear what I had done. I became the beast by entertaining love lost in confusion, distorted by fear and rejection. I lusted in place of love like a contagion, living life as a friend of the world's and an enemy of God. I said I believed in Jesus while rejecting his ways for life, furthermore ignorant to the significance of his death. I mocked and questioned the validity of scripture, foregoing God's ways for my own. My choice to follow myself instead of following Jesus left me hopelessly empty, wandering for a sense of purpose and belonging that no amount of money, career status, sex, worldly acceptance, or power could satisfy.

I've done my best to be as real and thorough as possible, as I've opened myself up to you in this way to divulge these stories about my life and the secret roots in my heart behind each one. If I have any regrets, it's of precious time lost. All of those years of back and forth we spent in confusion and blame, the years I spent treating people like the enemy, when it could have been time enjoyed loving each other. The root of the root was desiring to love according to my own ways, separate from the ways defined by the Author of Love. It simply does not work. Apart from the law of love, there is no unity, no respect for others, no generosity that seeks the well-being of another over one's self, no limit to what we will choose in effort to renounce heaven's reign over Rome's protagonist.

Two-weeks after returning from Iceland, I enrolled in seminary. I didn't even know what seminary was, taking the step out of trust in the person who provided it. I didn't know what to expect, except that I wanted a path that would allow me to glorify God with my life. Perhaps you remember some of that because you attended one of the orientation dinners with me. I imagine you saw me going down a road toward institutional religion that primarily resonated with hurt in your life. Not only was I a totally different person, but I was also headed in a very different direction than you had ever imagined. Well, it ended up being a totally different direction than I had ever imagined as well. The insides of the institutional church I experienced were as diseased as a cancerous gut. It made even corrupt corporate culture seem more safe, and late-night bar contenders feel more like accepting community. That seminary was a dangerous place to be, in the name of God. I was condemned for disagreeing with their desire to want God to be in the image of humans versus accepting the image God created us in. From my perspective, their consumption of God fostered a religion of people who portrayed a God who is selective, arrogant, distant, inconsistent, and hard of hearing. Images of broken people ... not of our unconditionally loving God, heavenly Father, Creator of heaven and earth. Perhaps the domino effect of God in the image of people has been the catalyst to every ism and divide that exists.

I ended up dropping out two years into the program, one year of which I took to discern the departure. There are many stories to tell from that time, hopefully for another day. In general, it was a sad yet enlightening season. Sad to witness people desperate to carry on an old covenant approach with a deafening focus on rituals and rules. Enlightening in a sense that catapulted me into deeper relationship with the cross. Institutional religion seems to neglect the fact that the curtain in the temple tore when Jesus was crucified. It negates the necessity of repentance, death to one's own life, and rebirth in Christ. It avoids the offensive nature of the Word, as if conviction is not the critical iron we need to separate us from our selfish desires to indulge in a liar. An indispensable measure of religious performance via institutional membership does have transformative power, to turn God into an obligation—coming dangerously close to dimming the light of Jesus's resurrection to life, ascension to heaven, and disbursement of his Holy Spirit upon earth so that we would have access to him at all times and in all places.

Perhaps even more disheartening is that the sins that I have confessed throughout these letters probably do not even sound like that big of a deal, because all of the behavior I have described is for the most part socially acceptable. Disrespecting parents, reliance on alcohol for reprieve, sexual immorality, divorce and affairs, resistance against authority, defiance against God, love of money, and focus on self-achievements are mere quintessential human experiences. It has even become offensive to say these things are wrong in many institutional religious settings, as so many houses of worship have started conforming to the world in fear the pews will empty and offerings will dwindle. Truth has been diluted by a feel-good inspirational message, proving to do nothing to change one's heart. It keeps God at a safe distance though. Where decisions about salvation are far enough off to worry about another day, and where it's easier to blame God for all that's wrong in the world rather than see our own personal responsibility in it. How guilty of that I was as well. I couldn't accept what Jesus did for me all those years in Sunday service because I could not see value in accepting that I was wrong. I wasn't even willing to hear it. And anything I did was certainly not wrong enough to be deserving of death. While it was a difficult message to eventually receive, I have found that is exactly what makes the good news—Good! Christianity as a religion is not about self-preserving, self-enhancing, self-advancing ways. It's about acknowledging self-destructive brokenness in need of a Savior. It's about understanding the hard heart conditions we are all born with and inviting Jesus to intervene with careful surgical precision, to transplant in us a new heart and a new identity. Without new hearts, there is simply no way we can live in this land and truly love God and our neighbors. I can say that with utmost confidence, that nothing in this world man or machine made will ever accomplish unity or banish hate. Only Jesus can do that. Only Jesus can change our hearts and fill us with love that innately desires to do good and love others more than ourselves.

I remember sitting on your couch in your old apartment, crying because I wanted to drop out of my candidacy at the seminary, while passionately sharing some of these thoughts I had with you about Jesus. You asked me to stop because you were not on the same level as me, yet said it was also what you loved most about me. I didn't know what that meant; however, it does make me wonder what you're thinking now. I never knew you to speak about your feelings in depth. Throughout all of the years we knew each other, you communicated your deepest feelings through musical lyrics or poems you personally wrote. I could always tell the vulnerabilities of your heart and mind by the text you shared. Words you could not say out loud, I suppose. I most enjoyed when you shared your poems with me. I don't know how many people had the same opportunity to read them; however, it made me feel very privileged and honored that you trusted me with it. At no time did they come with an explanation, which usually contributed to their preciousness. I still have the last one you sent to me. I kept it all these years, the one titled "I'll Miss You" about a badger and a honey bee. It opened with this:

> "I'll miss the way we'll never be," whispered the badger to the honey bee. "You fly too fast or am I too slow? Perhaps you simply disagree with where I go."

And it ended with this:

> "I'll miss the way we missed each other in this tiny wild land … for surly if we wanted more, there is something that could have been done. But now I crawl at a slower rate, still apart, paired with a blurry view. I suppose I will always miss the way it wasn't, between me and you."

My heart sank when I first read that, and it still does to this day. You were the badger, and I was the honey bee. Our hearts were worlds apart, dwelling in the same land, with our sole desire to be able to love one another. I knew at that point you were done. There would be no more back and forth, no more trying. It was about one year after you sent that to me that I ran into you at the church we used to go to together. It was exactly one week before I would drop out of seminary, but I didn't share that with you at the time. I watched you walk in, holding hands with a woman. I didn't think I could face you, so I tried to walk away before you saw me. Why you made the effort to approach me when you could have just as easily kept walking, I'll never know. I looked into your eyes, and all I could think of was how much I missed you. Like your poem said, I admit that I disagreed with where you were going. Even more so, I disagreed with where I was going. It was never my place to control your path, and any attempt to do that was certainly not love.

The group I was with happened to be sitting a few rows behind you. It was a scene seemingly orchestrated by God. The sermon message delivered just beyond your presence was about how Jesus cuts off every branch from our lives that bears no fruit, while he prunes those branches that do bear fruit so that they will be even more fruitful (John 15:2). Some of the branches that once connected us were cut from my life. I mourned that most of all, like your poem said, missing all of the ways it wasn't between me and you. I am sorry for all of the lies. I am sorry for how they hurt you. I was not afraid of saying goodbye, courage fueled only by knowing God's good plans for us.

Knowing there will be a day when we will find our footing together in this tiny, wild land. Where Love will finally conquer all, in its truest and purest sense. And where hearts will be humbled to repent of all the ways they resist God to focus on self. I walked out of that service with a humble heart. It was never about being in a romantic relationship with you, despite the fact that human understanding of love often leans that way. I had to let go of control, and I had to let go of you. It was never my place to change you. You changed me though. The beginning of my heart transformation became evident the day we met, when my hard and hopeless human heart began to desire love, in the cleanest and purest of ways. You see, you made me want to find the true definition of love, so that I could give it to you. I wanted to love so completely and so authentically that I searched the earth far and wide with a willingness to do whatever it took to find it. Even if it meant dying to obtain it.

There are things this world simply cannot help us with, no matter how many scientific theories or human rights movements persist. There is no medication in existence that can fill the deep voids in our hearts that long for love and belonging. There is no line of currency that can buy reconciliation between us or mend the vast amounts of hurts we all cause one another. There is no technology that can reverse time, that can take us back and allow us to undo the prideful stubbornness that caused us to miss one last chance for reparation before death stole the opportunity. No surgery can aid the ache in the heart that runs through the bones and penetrates a soul depraved of healing. There is nothing more infuriating than losing the chance, losing the opportunity to love, because of a plaque buildup of arrogance on our hearts. There is no other God with the power to forgive offenses. No other God willing to receive the punishment for a follower's disobedience. And there is no other God with the power to offer whole and free absolution to fear, anxiety, and shame. There is only one true God who can fill the void in our hearts with love and peace not circumstantially dependent but standing unshakable against life's harshest trials. Only one God created humans, and only that same God has the power to restore what he himself created that the world has attempted to corrupt and destroy. Only one God was willing to sacrifice his only Son, himself incarnate, in order to accomplish this. Despite the resistance against him, he still chose to take on the punishment we deserved in our place. Nowhere else in the universe does love like that exist. I never found myself changed by the power of shame. This irrational generosity, extended by Jesus, held the only power to free my deceitful human heart from hate, unforgiveness, disrespect, and sexual immorality. The things that promised to elevate me and in turn attempted to kill me, opening my eyes to see that God's will is not about a religious book of rules to follow. It's about exchanging an old heart for a new one.

The life I live now is one of true love and true religion. I have finally started to become who I always wanted to be: love, joy, peace, forbearance, kindness, goodness, faithfulness, gentleness, and self-control. This love appreciates and respects all humans, that no amount of self-awareness can train. This peace is constant and steady no matter what the circumstance or situation. This kindness, goodness, and gentleness naturally seeks to put the well-being and comfort of others first. This self-control is a firm footing, a kind of fortitude that no amount of meditation or self-help could ever instill. These are the characteristics that my heart naturally and authentically desires. I don't feel the need to be or do—I want only to love, forgive, reconcile, and give in all situations. Pride and resentment have been exchanged for forgiveness. Anger has been exchanged for faithfulness. Unrest has been exchanged for peace. Aggression has been exchanged for gentleness. Gluttony has been exchanged for self-control. And lust has been completely exchanged for love. With my whole heart, I testify that Jesus is the Messiah—he is the authority over heaven and earth, he is the forgiver of sins, he is the maker of new hearts, he is the true source of love and all things good. I think the greatest lesson I took from seminary was that giving my life to God was not a career choice—it was a relationship choice. A choice to choose love and life. A choice freely available to all people.

My new measures for success on this earthy walk are his, with eyes set on things above and a heart set on loving justice and walking humbly with my God. To live with integrity, humility, honesty, accountability, and authenticity. When I eventually returned to work, I opened every email with, "May this note find you well" and ended, "With peace and gratitude." A small notion to greet people with care and commit to collaborating in peace, with gratitude for God's good ways. It left a surprisingly significant impression on many people who otherwise receive a hundred emails a day demanding something from them or criticizing something they didn't do. It invited consensus and detested coercion. It introduced a leadership mindset of servant, ensuring demands of the other's job was aided first before my own. Extending peace and love, while achieving productive purpose as I sought to operate in the world as a regular person who happens to be a disciple of Jesus Christ, who also happened to experience life-altering love. I suppose my family was right all along, and settling down with a man would be the answer to my grief. If it wasn't already clear, the man's name is Jesus.

Love, too, has many disguises. Deceit is not one of them. While, thankfully, everything about me has changed, one thing remains the same—my untold love for you. If you find yourself one day thinking of me, with a heart willing to forgive … willing to receive the truth … write me back, please.

With peace and gratitude,
Chole